This book is dedicated to my family members, who have always shown me love and support through the good times and the bad times. Because of you, I never have to walk this road alone, and I have the strength to face any obstacle that is thrown in my direction.

This book is also dedicated to those who live with sickle cell and those who have lost their battle with sickle cell. No one else on this planet will ever know what it's like to live our lives and go through what we go through. We are a strong group of individuals who continue to inspire others through our strength, while showing the world just how strong we are. No matter what, never give up or lose hope—just keep fighting the fight because we will survive. It's our destiny!

# <u>CONTENTS</u>

# ACKNOWLEDGMENTS

Writing this book has truly been a dream come true for me, and there are many people I would like to thank.

First and foremost, thank you to my wife, Marissa Griffin, for being so loving, supportive, and understanding to me; it means the world to me, and I love you for that. Also, thank you for supporting me in all my endeavors and editing the rough draft of this book; it helped me out tremendously. Finally, thank you for being unrelenting in getting me to open up more about myself and my illness. You never let me off the hook because you were always putting me in a position to talk about it, whether it was with your family, coworkers, or friends. You are a very special person, and I'm glad to have you in my life.

To my parents, Linda and Jimmy Griffin, I love you and thank you for being such great parents to me, for raising me with the confidence to tackle whatever obstacle that presents itself, and never allowing me to use my illness as an excuse to give up. You taught me a lot, and I couldn't ask for anything more.

Thank you to my brother, Greg, and my sisters,

Jenell and Tanya Griffin, for always supporting me when I was sick in the hospital or sick at home. You are the only ones who really know what I went through and how it has strengthened us all and brought us closer together. To my nieces and nephews, Jalen, Tyler, Sydney, Kalynn, and Shalynn Griffin, I just want to say thank you for always coming to visit me while I was in the hospital. I love you all so much!

Thank you to the Alston family for always being there for me when I needed you. To me, you are more than just friends—you are family.

Thank you to Evelyn Brown for always taking my calls and sharing information with me on sickle cell; it has helped me become more knowledgeable about my condition. I am so appreciative of you, and I can't thank you enough.

To all the doctors and nurses over the years who have felt empathy for me, and have shared many personal conversations with me during my stays in the hospital, I give many thanks.

Finally, to all the other individuals who have played an instrumental role in my life and who stood beside me in my ups and downs, I give my sincere thanks. Last but not least, I would like to show my gratitude to the editors of this book for making it come together the way I had always envisioned it in my mind.

# FOREWORD

I wrestled back and forth many times with the idea of writing a book about living with sickle cell anemia, but deep down I just knew I had to write one. I wanted to show other people with this disease that they were not alone in this battle, and give them the strength and motivation to continue to live each day. I hoped by writing this book, I could inspire other people with sickle cell to speak out and open up, too. I also hoped that by bringing sickle cell to the forefront, more people would become aware of this global issue and be sparked to take action so together we can make a change. In this book, I will share with you what the pain is like for someone who has sickle cell and how it impacts our lives daily. I will also share with you the many struggles that may arise in our lives due, in part, to sickle cell. I want to give people with sickle cell another voice to be heard to ensure we all get the necessary medical attention and medical care we deserve. This book is to educate people about the effects of this chronic illness, and let people walk in my shoes so they can know what it is like for someone to live with sickle cell.

Many sleepless nights, I sat up in my bedroom

thinking about writing this book and wondering what people would think of me once it was finished. I was extremely nervous, to say the least, because this would be my first time truly opening up about my illness. My initial thoughts were what would I say and where to begin. Later on, I questioned whether or not I wanted to share my pain, my thoughts, and my feelings. Then one day, I finally looked myself in the mirror and I said, "Yes!" Once I decided to write the book, I promised myself that I would commit 100 percent and hold nothing back. For the sake of my readers, I hope that I have accomplished these goals.

The stories being told in this book are based on my real life experiences; in order to protect the identity of those involved, all names have been changed except where I have received permission to use them. My name is James Griffin III and this is my story of living with sickle cell anemia. There are many individuals living with sickle cell who have had vastly different experiences. My story is just one of many.

# CHAPTER 1

# BEGINNING

On March 28, 1981, I was born at Children's Hospital in Milwaukee, Wisconsin. I was born exactly two days after my father's birthday, and I was named after my father, and grandfather. I was the third child, and the only one to be born with sickle cell anemia. Before I came into the picture, my mother and father had my brother, Greg, and my sister Jenell. I was born four years after my brother and three years after my sister, so I always had someone to look up to. Then four years later, I was fitted with the shoes of being a big brother because my sister Tanya was born.

My parents were natives of Milwaukee; they spent their entire lives there, enjoying their youth and making livings for themselves before they would meet and go on to have four beautiful children. Milwaukee is the biggest city in Wisconsin; it has a lot of culture to it because it was home to people of all different backgrounds like the Germans, Polish, Italians, African Americans, Mexican Americans, and Greeks, just to name a few. To many, it is known as a blue-collar city, and back then it was a place where a lot people made a living working in factories or doing manual labor. In the summertime, many people came to visit Milwaukee, which was famous for its beer and breweries. As people gathered in the summer heat the festivals also became a huge attraction and soon it became a place where people could party and have a good time, as they enjoyed all the different tastes of the city. Because it sits on the shoreline of Lake Michigan during the winter, Milwaukee gets very cold and it snows a lot. In the summertime, the weather rarely gets above ninety degrees, but it is usually very humid. Many people loved it because it was a place where you could experience all four seasons, and it had a small-town atmosphere where you could raise a family. And that's exactly what my parents did, after they both got out of the army.

Before joining the army, my mother and father didn't know each other; their lives never even crossed paths until they both returned home. Even in the army, they were stationed in two different parts of the world. My mother was stationed in South Carolina and worked as a medic, training and learning how to provide medical care to military personnel. My father was stationed overseas in Germany, working as a mechanic, fixing tanks and Humvees. Oftentimes when my siblings and I were young, my mother would sit on the couch and tell us stories about the basic training she had to go through and all the equipment she had to wear. The first time I saw a picture of her dressed in her army fatigues holding a rifle, I erupted with laughter because it was so funny. It was something I couldn't imagine, but that sight only reinforced my thoughts about how tough of a woman she was. And that toughness within her was much needed when I was born, because she would have to be strong for me and all I endured with having sickle cell. My dad was also incredibly tough. His persona was very laid back and cool, but at the snap of a finger he could become commanding. The thing everyone knew him for most was his cooking and handyman work. He could make a five-star meal from scratch, which was very important in our home since we lived modestly at times. He could also fix anything around the house, so we nicknamed him Mr. Fix-It.

After spending years in the army, my mother returned to Milwaukee and continued to work in the medical field as a dental assistant. It was at this job that she met a coworker named Vivian, who would eventually introduce her to my father. By this time, my father had picked up a trade and was working as a welder. From the moment they met, they hit it off right away because they had a lot in common. However, the most important thing they had in common was that they each carried the gene for sickle cell. This was something neither one of my parents knew anything about, nor did it have any effect on them until after they got married and decided to have children. When I came along, they each passed down their sickle cell gene to me, which caused me to have sickle cell anemia.

So what is sickle cell anemia? To give you the definition according to the *Pain Sourcebook*, third edition:

> Sickle cell anemia is a serious condition in which the red blood cells can become sickle-shaped (shaped like a C). Normal red blood cells are smooth and round like a doughnut without a hole. They move easily through blood vessels to carry oxygen to all parts of the body. Sickle-shaped cells do not move easily through blood. They are stiff and sticky and tend to form clumps and get stuck in blood vessels. The clumps of sickle cells block blood flow in the blood vessels that

5

lead to the limbs and organs. Blocked blood vessels can cause pain, serious infection, and organ damage.

Sickle cell anemia may also be known as sickle cell disease or just sickle cell. In the United States alone, according to the National Institute of Health (NIH), sickle cell affects over seventy thousand people, and is the most common genetic disease, yet there is still a lack of awareness when it comes to this illness. Most people I talk to about sickle cell have the misconception that it only affects people of African descent, but sickle cell affects many different ethnic groups. According to the NIH, "Sickle cell anemia is most common in people whose families come from Africa, South or Central America (especially Panama), Caribbean Islands, Mediterranean countries (such as Turkey, Greece, and Italy), India, and Saudi Arabia."

Since sickle cell is a hereditary blood disorder, it is passed on from each parent to the child if both the parents are carriers of the disease. In my case, I received one sickle cell gene from my mother and one from my father. This in turn gave me two sickle cell genes, which is the combination that causes sickle cell anemia. Each of my parents had the sickle cell trait, but neither one of them was ever aware of it. In the early 1970s, knowledge and understanding of the illness, especially in the African American community, was even lower than it is today. More than likely, the only way a person would know if he or she carried the trait was if someone in the family had sickle cell. Once one family member was diagnosed, the doctors would do blood tests on the others.

So what were the chances of getting it? Each person carries two genes in their body and will pass on one of those genes to his or her baby. If a person has the sickle cell trait, he or she will have one (A) and one (S) gene. The (A) represents the normal red blood cell and the (S) represents the sickle cell gene. Now, if two people with sickle cell trait have a child together, there are always four possible combinations of red blood cell genes that the baby can inherit:

- 25 percent chance that the baby will inherit two sickle cell genes and have the disease;
- 25 percent chance that the baby will inherit two normal genes and not have the disease or trait;
- 50 percent chance that the baby will inherit one normal gene and one sickle cell gene. In that case, the baby will not have the disease, but he or she will have the sickle cell trait like his or her parents.

### Chance of Passing on the Sickle Cell Gene

| | |
|---|---|
| Baby inherits<br>• S from Mother<br>• S from Father<br>Has sickle cell disease and can pass it on to his or her children | Baby inherits<br>• A from Mother<br>• A from Father<br>Does not have sickle cell disease or trait, so cannot pass on the disease to his or her children |
| Baby inherits<br>• A from Mother<br>• S from Father<br>Does not have sickle cell disease but carries the sickle cell trait and can pass it on to his or her children | Baby inherits<br>• S from Mother<br>• A from Father<br>Does not have sickle cell disease but carries the sickle cell trait and can pass it on to his or her children |

   I have sickle cell SS, the most severe form of sickle cell anemia. There are several other forms of sickle cell.

Sickle cell SC and S Beta thalassemia both are considered by doctors to be milder types of sickle cell. However, they still can have the same serious symptoms as the most severe form. In my opinion, all the forms are very serious; if not treated properly, they can cause damage to tissue and major organs, and can also lead to death. Sickle cell usually starts to show in people after six months of age. The first signs of the illness could be swelling of the hands and feet, which is known as hand and foot syndrome. However despite the symptoms that come along with having the illness, people who have sickle cell look fairly healthy, which is why it can be such a hard illness to detect.

My mother told me that I had jaundiced eyes when I was born, but the nurse reassured her that it was OK because jaundice was a common condition for newborn babies. Never in her wildest dreams could she imagine that the jaundice would be a sign of something worse and a common trait in me throughout my life.

I had my first sickle cell crisis before I could walk, and they would continue from then on. A crisis is the hallmark of sickle cell; it consists of severe chronic pain in any location of the body, wherever blood flows—the chest, legs, arm, back and so on. A crisis can be brought on by a decrease in oxygen levels in the body due to overexertion, temperature changes, fever, stress, high altitude, or dehydration.

I was first diagnosed with sickle cell when I was two years old. At the time, no one in my family was educated or knowledgeable about sickle cell. However, after I was born, they would become students of sickle cell and come to learn about it through many trips with me to the hospital and doctor's office. Since I was too young to remember the specific details of how my sickle cell was discovered, I have called upon my mother to share her story of that day when we found out.

**Momma's Story:**

James was two years old when we found out
that he had sickle cell. He was in his walker
bouncing around the house, playing like
your typical toddler, when suddenly we
heard him screaming and crying. My
husband and I were sitting on the couch in
the living room with our other two children,
Greg and Jenell, as they played on the floor
around him. After I heard James crying, I
ran over to him to see what was wrong.
Initially, I didn't notice anything, so I just
held him in my arms to try and calm him
down, but I couldn't. The screams continued
to persist, so I looked him over again, and
that's when I noticed his hand was visibly
swollen. To me it looked like a latex glove
filled with water. When I saw James's hand
swollen and puffy, the first thing that came
to my mind was that he had accidently
banged his hand on a wall while he was
playing around the kitchen. Oddly enough, I
hadn't heard anything, so that made me
think otherwise.

Hours later, after the swelling went down,
my husband and I decided we were going to
take him to the hospital the next day, so he
could be evaluated by a doctor. In the
doctor's office, we explained to the doctor
what had happened, and how we thought
that James might have hit his hand on a wall
while playing in his walker. By then, the
swelling was completely gone down and

there were no signs of a broken bone, so the doctor didn't feel the need to take any X-rays of the hand. Instead, the doctor decided to run some blood tests on him as a precaution. The next day, after the results came back from the blood test, we were instructed to schedule another appointment to follow up with the doctor regarding the results. In this appointment, the doctor broke the news to us that James had the inherited blood disorder sickle cell anemia.

I had heard sickle cell mentioned once or twice when I was younger, and later discovered that my oldest sister, Dorothy, had it before she passed away from complications of the disease, but I didn't know exactly what it was. Keep in mind that was in the 1940s, when they knew even less about it. But later on, through James, we would come to find out firsthand what it meant to have it, and the things that he would have to endure because of it. When I was told James had sickle cell anemia, I was heartbroken and deeply saddened by the news because I didn't know what to expect from it. I also didn't want to picture him in pain his whole life. I just wanted the best for him, and prayed that he would be all right. That being said, I didn't panic or get upset or feel any guilt; I just wanted to know what it was and what it all entailed.

That's when the doctors explained to us that it was an inherited blood disorder where the hemoglobin in the red blood cells are sickle shaped and can cause a great deal of pain when they don't get enough oxygen. However, the doctor said the pain could be managed with proper care and treatment. In order for someone to be born with this condition, both parents had to be carriers of the sickle cell trait. In James's case, he received a sickle gene from me and a sickle gene from my husband, and that is how he ended up with it. There was so much information for me to take in all at once. It was hard for me to keep it together, but I had my husband there to lean on for strength and support. I took a deep breath, pulled myself together, and said, "OK, we will take it from here." This was a part of life, and we vowed to treat and love James the same as the rest of our children, no matter what.

Even though sickle cell was hard on me, I cannot fathom what they must have been going through as parents. To hear the words "sickle cell," and not know exactly what to expect, must have been frightening and heartbreaking for them.

For me, sickle cell would be a very long struggle filled with a lot of pain and a lot of questions. The most important question of all of course was, "Why me?" The answer to that question will never be known, but I do believe that it was just what God had in store for me, and if I didn't have the strength to handle it, he would not have placed it upon me.

Through the years leading to adulthood, I have learned how to deal with my sickle cell and handle the pain when it comes. I have also learned so much about myself and about others. I have come to the conclusion that there are genuinely good people out there who care and are willing to help you in any way they can. This is the first time I have really spoken out publicly about my condition and the way it has made me feel. Until this point, I have always kept my feelings deep down inside of me. I have shown no emotion at all about living with sickle cell except behind closed doors. Today, I no longer have any of the guilt that I placed on myself or the feeling of shame that was always synonymous with sickle cell for me. As best as I could, I have always tried to remain upbeat and optimistic through it all, keeping a smile on my face. For that alone, I can thank the best support system anyone could have asked for—my family.

# CHAPTER 2

# <u>BEING A KID</u>

As a kid, I was always pretty shy and timid, especially around adults like my aunties, my uncles, and my dad's friends, but around my peers I had no problem opening up, and I would open up rather quickly. I was always the kid who tried to make everyone laugh once I felt comfortable around you. It wasn't unusual to find me doing something silly or pulling a little prank on my younger sister, Tanya, and her friends while they spent the night over at our house. They say laughter is good for the soul and the best medicine, so maybe that's why I enjoyed being such a jokester. Laughing made me feel good, and I just wanted to see everyone else smiling, happy, and feeling good, too. When it came down to talking about sickle cell, there were only a few times that I can recall ever being vocal about having it, otherwise I hid the condition. Back then if you asked me if I had sickle cell, I would deny it in a heartbeat.

Growing up, I remember playing outside the house

with the other kids from my neighborhood and, compared to the other kids my age, I would always be the smallest one. A lot of the kids would always say that I was so skinny or that I didn't look my age, but none of it really mattered to me. I would just shake it off and continue playing. As a game, some kids would take their hands and wrap them around my wrist to see how far up my arm they could go before their fingers couldn't stay closed anymore. It was annoying to me—I hated to wear shorts or short sleeves around them in the summertime because of my size. A common trait in children with sickle cell is they are often smaller, lighter, and thinner than their peers. They also become tired more easily when involved in vigorous activities. As a kid, my energy level was high, and I loved to play nonstop at the park or playground with my friends, but sometimes I found it hard to keep up. After playing a short time outside, I would be huffing and puffing, and start getting tired before all the other kids. They would find it a little hard to believe, making comments like, "You're smaller than me, and I'm not even tired," or "How can you be tired already when we just started playing?" They all wondered, but I never said anything—I just kept quiet.

The first time I admitted to anyone that I had sickle cell, I was about eight years old. It happened one day while I was running around chasing my friend, Brandon, as we were playing a game of tag in his front yard. After running in circles and chasing him around for countless minutes, I stopped for a break to sit on his front steps so I could try to catch my breath. I remember Brandon and his sister, Claudia, were standing around me with my sister Jenell, my brother, Greg, and a couple of other kids from the neighborhood.

As I was sitting and everyone else was standing in the front yard of his house, Brandon asked me, "How come you get tired so quick all the time?"

Without a hitch, I looked at him and told him matter-of-factly, "I have sickle cell." Everyone who was huddled around us paused for a second, including my brother and sister.

Jenell blurted out loudly, "No, he doesn't! He's just joking and playing with you guys, so don't believe what he's telling you." I wasn't joking—I was dead serious! No one really took notice of what I had said, but after that interaction I chose to remain silent for the rest of the time until I got home.

When we got home, Jenell squealed to my mother that I was telling everyone I had sickle cell, so mother had a long talk with me about sharing family business. From then on, if I let a secret slip or told on my brother or sister for doing something wrong, Jenell would say, "You know you can't tell James anything, because he has a mouth as big as the Pacific Ocean."

It baffled me, because I was a kid who was opening up, telling the truth, and being honest. However, my mother was very protective about us telling our family business, so I had to listen to her and live by her rules. And she wanted *absolutely* no one to know about my health. My father, on the other hand, could not have cared less, and he wasn't going to hide anything. If I was in the hospital, he would tell all my friends and give them my room number so they could come and see me. I hated that the most. It was obvious my parents each had their own perspectives on how to handle my situation. It was like night and day. And in some sort of way, I think this all was starting to have an effect on me.

Later on, I took to my mother's approach about

silence, and it became much harder for me to open up. Eventually, I put up barriers and would not talk to anyone about my illness. I never knew why my mother was so protective of speaking the truth about my health when I was a kid, but later on in life I would come to appreciate that she continued to help me keep it hidden from all my friends. Together we went to great lengths not to let anything be known, and making stories up became the norm for us. Though my sickle cell was invisible, and I looked perfectly healthy walking down the street, the one thing that I couldn't hide was my imperfect, jaundiced eyes.

Jaundice is a symptom of the illness and is a very common trait among people with sickle cell. It is caused by the red bloods cells breaking down more rapidly than the liver can filter them out. Bilirubin, which is a yellow substance found in red blood cells, builds up in the body from these broken-down cells and then leaks out into the bloodstream, causing jaundice or the yellowish color you see in the eyes or skin. Not everyone with sickle cell has jaundice of the eye, but it can be a huge telltale sign that you have the condition. Jaundice occurred a lot in me, especially when I was going through a crisis or coming out of a crisis. When the whites of my eyes were jaundiced, sometimes my attitude would become more withdrawn, and I would get down on myself. But when they weren't, I was in high spirits. Jaundice was the one thing that I resented most about having the illness, and that made it harder for me to accept it. They say the eyes are the windows to our souls and, in my case, they were also the window to my health because they were the first thing people noticed when they looked at me. I hated it with a passion, because I had a harder time covering up the fact that something was wrong. Many times when I was sick and my eyes were jaundiced, people would just stare at me like I was a walking zombie straight out of a horror flick.

If I went outside when my eyes were jaundiced, I would get bombarded with a million and one questions. It seemed like a personal attack. It made me just want to shut down and not say a word because I couldn't take all of the attention.

People would stop me all the time and ask, "Why are your eyes yellow?"

I would say, "They just get like that," then walk away.

Then someone else would say to me, "Your eyes are yellow. When was the last time you been to the doctor?"

Again, I would be brief and say, "A while, but I'm fine!" and keep on walking.

Then there were times people even made rude comments to me about them, saying things like, "Why do you have that weird yellow color in your eyes? They look like a cat!"

It was another blow to my self-esteem, but I would just try to remain unfazed by it. I would just nod, smile, and take off. The list just went on and on, and it was the same thing every day. To deal with it all, I would use video games as my escape. I would just sit in my room and play for hours and hours. But when it was time for me to leave the house every day, before I got dressed I would look in the mirror to check my eyes and see how they looked. "Are they jaundiced or not?" I would ask myself. "If they are, how bad are they? Are they very noticeable?" It stayed on my mind constantly, and there was nothing that I could do to change how they looked, so I tried my best just to ignore it all.

The only other time that I spoke out about my health, I was at the park with my family, enjoying another holiday. My family always went to Smith Park to celebrate the Fourth of July and watch the fireworks with all my relatives. It was an all-day event for us, and we spent the day eating, lighting firecrackers, and having a good time. We would get up early in the morning, put on our new clothes, and head over to the park so we could all hang out. My dad would begin barbequing while my mother, my aunties, and my uncles would be talking and playing card games at the picnic tables. All of the kids would be scattered around the park playing and enjoying the festivities. As we played at the park by the swings, one of the kids there noticed my eyes were jaundiced behind the big, round glasses I had sitting on my face.

He asked me, "How come your eyes are yellow?"

With excitement in my voice, I told him, "I have sickle cell anemia."

The next thing I knew, all the kids started running away from me while I was chasing them trying to explain that it wasn't contagious. It was embarrassing, shameful, and hurtful, all at the same time. The reaction of those kids ripped through my skin and tore me apart like a great white shark. I was crying on the inside. I couldn't picture a time in my life when I was more upset. My cousin Perry was very upset by it, too. It made him so mad that they were ridiculing me; he wanted to go over to the other kids and fight them for picking on me.

A lot of times, what we go through early in life can shape our future and have a huge effect on us as we get older. It can change the ideas we have, the way we think, and how we see the world. For me, going through these negative experiences as a kid, every time I opened up and spoke out about my illness just chipped away at my self-esteem. Even worse, the way other people responded only made me want to keep everything bottled up. I think, had my experiences been more positive, and people hadn't judged me, maybe I would have been more open about sickle cell throughout my life. But everything we go through in life can be a learning experience and should be used as a tool to teach us better the next time we are faced with the same situations.

# CHAPTER 3

# **<u>SCHOOL</u>**

**B**ack when I was in elementary school, I can remember being absent from school for weeks at a time. I would be in school for a week or a month; then a crisis would hit me, and I would have to miss school for a week or so. My sickle cell had caused me to be in and out of school regularly, and my teachers all took this into account as a legitimate excuse in regards to my attendance. Before the start of every school year, my mother would be very vocal in communicating to all my teachers, my counselors, and my principals about my health, so everyone was well informed about the possibility of me missing school.

There were also certain accommodations that were made to prevent me from getting sick at school. I was allowed to carry a water bottle, go to the bathroom when I needed to, and rest in gym class. Pain episodes were unpredictable, so everyone had to be aware of that and understand how it could affect my attendance. But my attendance wasn't the only thing they needed to be aware of; they also needed to be alert for any sudden changes in my behavior. Strokes and acute chest syndrome (sickle cells trapped in the lungs) are both serious complications of the condition and can occur in children as young as six. Everyone knew if I was in pain, not to hesitate to send me to the office so I could call home and be picked up from school.

At least once a month, I had to visit the school secretary because of a crisis. No matter how it was triggered or what part of my body was affected, I needed to follow the same routine: I would let my teacher know, and she would send me down to the office where I would tell the secretary that I wasn't feeling well. She would hand me the telephone, so I could call home. At this point my mother was working from home as a childcare provider, so she was always there to accept my calls. When she picked up the telephone, I would begin to tell her I didn't feel good, I was sick, and I needed to come home.

She would ask me, "James, what's wrong?"

I would say to her, "Momma, my back is hurting now."

She would ask, "Can you stick it out and finish the day, or wait until after lunch and see how you feel?" My mother always tried to get me to stay in school because my parents were big on school, and they cared immensely about our education. When I told her I couldn't stay any longer because my back was hurting too bad and I couldn't sit still, she would say to me, "OK. Well, I will tell them to send you home."

I would hand the secretary the telephone, and she would hang up and call a bus, so that I could be dropped off at home. The conversation between my mother and me only lasted about two minutes, but it was long enough to determine whether or not I was staying in school.

When I spoke on the telephone, the principle, Mr. Robinson, would always be looking on from behind the desk in his office. He understood my condition very well and told me one day he had a family member who was facing the same battles as me, but I never knew who. I was very fortunate he knew about my condition. Throughout my schooling most of my teachers never had a clue what sickle cell was, but his compassion and understanding worked in my favor.

For example, one day during fitness week in gym, I had such a severe crisis from all the running around and physical exertion that I couldn't make it back to class to finish the rest of the day. It felt like my body was being squeezed in a huge compactor because all my muscles were cramping at the same time, and the pain was unbearable. Mr. Robinson saw me in the office sprawled out on the bench from obvious pain, so he wasted no time and decided to drive me home from school at that moment.

On the ride home, he said to me, "James, I'm going to pray for you and hope things get better." He never spoke much or showed his emotions, but on that day, on the way home, I got to see a different side of him.

Since kids are the only ones who can relate how they are feeling, I know a lot of times some adults may be skeptical and think the child is playing a "sick role" to get special attention. I will say that you have to trust the kid, monitor the kid, and get to know the kid because he or she is the only one who can tell you exactly how it feels. The pain from a sickle cell crisis is as painful to a child as it is to an adult. Never once have I taken it upon myself to fake being sick for the attention, the sake of staying home, or to get out of school. I enjoyed school too much and wanted to stay on track while I was healthy and capable. Whenever I was out of school, I would miss an obscene amount of work assignments, and the homework would pile up neck high. But even though my work load was heavy at times because of my absences, I never fell too far behind, failed a class, or had to be enrolled in any kind of special-education classes. With a little extra time and help, if needed, I managed to stay on top of my grades and finish with the rest of my class. Despite the myth that sickle cell can cause you to have a learning disability or affect the way children learn, there is no correlation between the two.

I grew up in a household where my parents valued education and showed us by attending our parent teacher conferences, making sure we did our homework, and attending other school functions. They stayed on us constantly about our schooling, and we had to go to school every day. It didn't matter to my parents if there was a blizzard outside or six feet of snow on the ground; if the school was open, we were there bright and early. Every morning when it was time for me to go to school, my mother would come into my room and flip the light on as she yelled out, "Rise and shine!" Once I heard that, I had to get up out of bed so I could get dressed and ready for the school bus to pick me up.

On days when my father would get me up for school, he would just come into my room, turn the light on, and say, "James, wake up. It's time for you to go to school." Then I would roll out of bed and start picking out my clothes for the day. Sometimes I hated for my dad to send me off to school, because he would make me wear dress slacks that all my classmates called my church pants. And when I wore them, everyone said I looked like I was going to sing in a church choir. I guess he figured I needed to change it up, since I would only wear my two favorite pairs of jeans throughout the week. But as far as the teasing went, that was all I dealt with in class. My teachers never allowed any teasing to go on about my health when they were around. At the beginning of the year, they would always give a speech to the class about being different.

However, when I got to junior high and high school, it was a different atmosphere. I would get teased often and hear comments about my eyes being jaundiced.

To get to and from school, I always rode the school bus. It would pick me up blocks from my house. In the second grade, during the winter time, I remember treading through hills of snow all bundled up with my brother, Greg, and older sister, Jenell. I would have on my winter coat, hat, gloves, and a scarf around my neck to keep me warm as I stood outside at the bus stop. While I waited for the bus to come, I would catch snowflakes with my tongue and play in the snow. But eventually, the long walks and the freezing cold weather would prove to be too much for me, because my ankles would start hurting, and I would have a crisis from being in the cold. This led my mother to call the school and ask for a separate bus to pick me up in front of my house. The cold weather affects people with sickle cell because it drops the body temperature and slows down the blood flow, so the red blood cells have a tendency to move sluggishly through the veins, sticking together more easily, and triggering a crisis.

I attended the same school as my brother and sisters, so each time I would miss a day, they all had their turns going to my classroom to pick up my homework from my teachers. Because my siblings were coming in and out of my classroom picking up my homework assignments while I was out, my teachers got to know each of them very well. From then on, every time they would see my brother and sisters around the school, they would say, "Hi." When I reached the sixth grade, my final year of elementary school, my younger sister, Tanya, would take on sole responsibility for picking up my assignments. She had permission to leave her classroom and come to mine before the end of each school day to pick up all the homework that I missed. The moment that I started to feel better, I would work to complete my assignments for the past days or weeks. After I returned to school, I would hear from the other students in my class about Tanya coming in to my classroom. The boys especially would all be excited to tell me stories about her and give me every little detail. I found out which one of my friends liked her and thought she was cute, along with a rundown of what clothes she was wearing, as if I needed to know.

Being absent from school never had a negative effect on me when it came to my grades because I loved school, I love to read, and I loved learning new things. My favorite subjects were math and reading, and I could catch on and learn new things quickly. My mother constantly told me I was very smart because I would always finish my homework with no help and get good grades on all my assignments. When I was in the hospital, it became a normal routine for me to finish my homework there; it was something I didn't have to think twice about or have to be forced to do. Once I returned to school, I was never teased or made fun of by the other students. They always just asked me, "Where have you been?" and said they were glad to see me back.

In the classroom, my teachers never shared my health with the class or treated me any different from the other students. I was expected to complete all the same assignments and tests, and I received the same punishments.

My all-time favorite teacher was my sixth grade teacher, Mr. Williamson. He was very funny, he seemed to care the most about his students, and he always kept me included in activities while I was out sick. I remember one day when I absent from his classroom and sick in the hospital with pneumonia, he came to visit me. Without any kind of notice, he stopped in to my hospital room and surprised me with a visit. I had no idea he was coming, so the look on my face said it all. When I saw him walking through the door, my eyes got as big as an owl because I was so shocked. I also felt a little embarrassed because I was caught in the middle of eating a cherry Popsicle, so my mouth was all covered in red. I didn't know if I should continue eating it or toss it! But Mr. Williamson just grinned and waited for me to finish. He came later in the evening, right around the time visiting hours were winding down, so I was not expecting anyone at all by then. But even if had I been, out of all the people I could think of, he was probably the last person I would expect to come visit me. Not because I did not think he cared about me as a student, but because I did not know that he cared that much as a teacher. It never would have dawned on me that a teacher of mine would come to visit me while I was sick in the hospital, so I was delighted to see him there and enjoyed his company. Mr. Williamson stayed for at least an hour, sitting in the reclining chair next to me, talking. His stay felt like it went by in a flash because there were no interruptions from the nurses or nurses' aides, and to my surprise my IV didn't even beep once or make a sound. The only noise I heard came from the TV that was on in the background.

Before I knew it, it was already time for him to go and he was packing up his things to leave. That was when he told me that my classmates were all waiting for me to come back to class and hoped that I felt better real soon.

That put a huge smile on my face and made me feel good inside. As he stood up to leave, he opened a bag he had brought in with him and pulled out an official USA Olympic basketball cap. He flicked it open and placed it on top of my head. Then he said, "James, this is yours, champ. Now get better." Wow! I could not believe it! I was so happy I continued to thank him as I shook his hand goodbye.

For the rest of the school year, that night stuck in my mind because it meant so much to me. By the time I got back to school, I wasn't sure if anyone in the classroom even knew about it, but I never mentioned a thing. What I took away from that night was that he cared about me, not only as a student but as an individual. He didn't have to come and see me, but he did anyway. Outside of my family, Mr. Williamson was the first person ever to visit me in the hospital, and the only teacher who ever visited me in the hospital. Like footprints in the sand, that left a lasting impression on me.

When you're a kid dealing with an illness as chronic as mine was, the last thing you want to do is be stuck in the hospital. It feels like you're trapped, and you're just waiting to be discharged. It can be rough when you're missing school or missing the time to hang out and play with your friends. That's when you can start to see the difference in you. When the sun was out, I knew all my friends were outside enjoying it and having fun without me—that made me feel sad. Many times, I would get out of my hospital bed, walk over to the window, and just stare outside at the scenery. As I watched the sun beam on the sidewalks and buildings, I would have a whirlwind of thoughts swirling through my head like, "Where would I be if it wasn't for this illness?"

But it was times like these, when guests showed up,

that made me forget about the reality of my crisis and kept me feeling alive and bubbly. I can honestly say that there is so much good that comes from having visitors. They give you that comfort and support along with an extra boost to make you want to get better. It makes you feel good to see that someone cares about you, and you're not alone. Ever since my nieces and nephews were born, they have all come to see me in the hospital, and every time they come, they just brighten up my day.

# CHAPTER 4

# **THE CLINIC**

$E$arly on, I had no understanding of what sickle cell was. I just remember being in pain a lot, and going back and forth to the hospital when I would get sick. I was born with sickle cell SS—the most severe form—and I started off getting crises at the age of two. From then on, crisis and pain became a way of life for me.

Although much of my early childhood is a bit hazy, I still can picture being in the hospital when I was younger; those memories are deeply embedded in my mind and will never go away. I can remember sharing hospital rooms with other patients when I was a toddler, as my parents kept me company and held me in their arms to console me when I would have crying spells from the pain. Many times when I was in the hospital, I would get a ton of stuffed animals from the volunteers who would walk along the children's floor of the hospital with a cart filled with things to give to all of the sick little kids. Whenever people entered my section of the room, I would always be looking at them from the view of my crib, with an IV attached to my foot.

This was my early introduction to sickle cell. As I got old enough to comprehend what was wrong with me, I started to receive an explanation for what was causing the excruciating pains I went through. But even as it was explained to me, there was nothing that could prepare me for everything else that came along with having my illness—like spending time in the hospital on my birthday, missing holidays with my family because I was stuck in the hospital, or even knowing how the pain would continually affect me. Those were all things I had to find out on my own as I grew up with my "best friend" sickle cell.

My earliest recollections of being told that I had sickle cell, and what that meant, came during a visit to the sickle cell clinic at Children's Hospital in Milwaukee. I was about seven years old when I was first told that I had inherited this genetic blood disorder. This was a moment of clarity that gave me an explanation for everything that was going on inside my body.

The sickle cell clinic in Milwaukee was a comprehensive clinic, which meant that it specialized in providing quality care for all the sickle cell patients. At my first appointment there, I would meet with a nurse, a physician, and a social worker. After the nurse had charted my height and weight, and taken my vitals, the social worker would educate me on my disorder.

I was always a very curious kid with a thirst for knowledge, so as soon as I was told about my disorder by the social worker, the first words out of my mouth were, "How many other people have it?" It was definitely a question that took the social worker by complete surprise. Nevertheless, she fumbled through her papers, and proceeded to give me the statistics.

She told me that, according to the NIH, between seventy thousand and one hundred thousand people in the United States are affected by sickle cell anemia, mainly African Americans. It was astounding to hear that I was part of these statistics. Knowing those numbers didn't change my situation, but it gave me peace of mind to know that I was not alone. To date, sickle cell (which was identified in 1910) is the largest and most common genetic illnesses there is in the United States.

After all the questions and talking, the social worker concluded that portion of the appointment and in came a new face. It was a nurse named Evelyn; when she walked into the room and introduced herself to me, she was very outgoing and she spoke with such passion and clarity. As I greeted her, I remember being nervous and shy, but her openness toward me was so authentic, it made me feel as if I had known her already. I thought of her as being like an auntie. This was the first time I had met Evelyn, and if you had told me then that she would become a necessity for maintaining my health well into adulthood, I never would have guessed it.

Evelyn was a registered nurse and the sickle cell coordinator; she helped manage the care of well over a hundred sickle cell patients in the clinic. She covered all the basics of sickle cell with me, and informed me about the symptoms I could have as a result of my illness. For instance, she gave me all the potential warning signs of a stroke. A stroke can happen when the sickled red blood cells block the supply of oxygen to the brain resulting in a severe crisis in the head. The warning signs are a numb feeling in the face, or the face drooping on one side, along with slurring of speech and an unusual pounding headache.

She said, "James, I want you to tell your mother to call 911 immediately if you ever experience any of these symptoms, because this is a very serious complication that could be potentially fatal!" I sat in the hard plastic chair with my eyes glued to her. I was so terrified that I wanted to make a dash for the door, so my tender ears didn't have to hear anymore. But this was only the beginning, and with that in mind, I hoped that the rest of the appointment would be more positive.

According to *The Iron Disorders Institute Guide to Anemia*, "About 10 percent of children with sickle cell disease have strokes...the peak incidence is between four and six years of age...although strokes usually occur without warning, they are occasionally preceded by severe headaches or deterioration of school performance. The sudden appearance of a limp in a child with sickle cell disease warrants careful evaluation for a neurologic cause." Early testing can be done on kids who started to have extremely severe crises at an early age, using a machine called a transcranial Doppler ultrasound (TCD) to see if they were at risk for strokes. I never had to have this procedure because my case appeared normal.

Another symptom of the illness, one that only affects males, was something called priapism. Before this appointment I had never heard that funny sounding word, so I had to refrain from chuckling the first time I heard it pronounced. But priapism is no laughing matter. Evelyn explained that it's a serious symptom that affected the penis in males with sickle cell. It is caused when sickle cells block the blood flow out of the penis, creating a painful obstruction that leads to an extremely painful erection. If not promptly treated, it can potentially damage the penis and lead to impotence. In some cases, treatment could be surgery or just pain relief medication. Priapism is more likely to happen by age twelve, but it could also happen as an adult.

The information just poured in and flooded my mind. It was a lot for me to take in at once, and I wished I didn't have to worry about these complications at age seven, but it was information I needed to know.

As the appointment continued, I remained seated in my chair like a statue while Evelyn went on to tell me about acute chest syndrome. Acute chest syndrome is the sickling of the red blood cells in the tiny vessels of the lungs. It can occur suddenly or with an infection or fever, and could cause shortness of breath, as well as damage to the lungs. She stressed that we should seek medical attention for extreme pain in the chest, so that it could be monitored carefully, because prevention and early treatment were essential to long-term health.

Those were just a few of the symptoms we covered in the office on that day. There were many more, and each time I came back I would learn about new ones, like eye problems, pulmonary hypertension, avascular necrosis, and leg ulcers. Not every person with sickle cell experiences these symptoms, since it affects everyone differently, but it is important to know about these symptoms because it could make the difference in sustaining your health.

After discussing the symptoms, Evelyn gave me my immunizations. Every year that I came to the clinic, I would have to get vaccinations, which were usually given to me when my appointment was all finished. Vaccinations were very important to me because they helped the body fight infections and build defenses against viruses and germs. Because people with sickle cell have weaker immune systems than the average person, we rely much more on vaccinations to prevent us from getting sick. It was recommended that I get mine every year and not miss getting them. I also was put on penicillin and stayed on it until I reached eighteen.

The scheduled clinic appointments were always one hour long, because I had to see a nurse, a physician, a counselor, and then Evelyn. It made for a long day. While I waited for the next person to come into the room and see me, I would run around and play in the makeshift play area the clinic had set up. This kept me busy, and I could interact with the other kids who were there.

Sometimes I wasn't able to make it out to the clinic for my annual vaccinations, and Evelyn would drive to my house to give them to me. One time I remember, she came in the middle of winter when the weather was blistering cold, and the sidewalks were all covered in snow. As she stood at the front door of my house, she was covered from head to toe in layers of clothes.

Evelyn did a lot for us sickle cell patients and, besides my mother, she was one of the most kindhearted, caring people I knew. I'm forever thankful for her because, without a shadow of doubt, she has helped me have a better understanding of my health and ensured I got the best care. Many times, we meet people like Evelyn and we take them for granted, but without them our lives would not be the same.

When I was about ten years old, I started going to these Christmas parties every year that were held for the sickle cell patients and their families. They were coordinated by Evelyn and took place in a big warehouse building on the north side of town. I absolutely loved the Christmas parties, and I always had a ball. They played music for us to dance to, there were food and drinks, and we got to interact with other people who had sickle cell and their families. For me, that was the best part about it, because the only time I ever saw anyone with sickle cell was at the clinic every year or when I was in the hospital. These parties were always great to go to because they took my mind off of everything for that moment; by being around other children with sickle cell outside of a hospital setting, I felt a great a sense of belonging. After the food was done being served, it would be time for Santa Claus; we each had a turn to tell him what we wanted for Christmas. Then after it was all done, each sickle cell patient got to come up—according to age—and pick out a present from a stack of toys that was laid out across the floor. If there were any presents left over, they would always let the younger siblings of the patients come up and pick out a present also. My little sister, Tanya, loved coming to this event every year with me, and she was always lucky enough to leave with a gift in hand, too. My mother and my sisters always came along with me. We went every year until the clinic could no longer sponsor it, because of the lack of funding.

By the time I reached junior high, I went to a weekly sickle cell support group just for teens. This group was also put together by Evelyn and a couple of other nurses from the sickle cell clinic. In this support group, I met with other teens living with sickle cell, and we would discuss different topics related to our health. A van would pick me up from my house in the evening and drive me and the others it had picked up to the meeting, which took place in a conference room in Children's Hospital. In these meetings, we talked about coping strategies for dealing with pain, how we were being treated in the hospitals, and what changes we would like to see that could help us in the future. It was definitely a chance for us to vent our frustrations and get a lot of things off our chests, and I found it very therapeutic. I also gained a lot of insight from them. A couple of times, they had guest speakers for us who were also living with the illness. I think these guest speakers were the highlight for me; I was extremely excited about it because I could see someone older who had been through what I was going through, and who made it through all the obstacles we face, despite having sickle cell. That gave me inspiration. I could picture myself doing just as well twenty years down the line. The guest speakers shared stories about their lives, and gave us some useful advice on how to stay healthy, like exercising and eating healthy, as well as the importance of staying away from drugs and alcohol. The meetings lasted an hour, but they always seemed to go by so quickly, since we were all engaged and having fun. As the night concluded the van would take us back home, and I would wait for the next time to go. I loved the meetings because they did so much for my self-esteem. It felt good to be around people who were just like me. I did not have to worry about facing any judgments, since we were all dealing with the same thing. Those were the times that were good for me in dealing with my illness, because I was involved in the support group, they had the Christmas parties going on, and I was still going to the sickle cell clinic every year.

After I turned eighteen, I no longer went to the sickle cell clinic, and I ended up losing touch with Evelyn. In those years my crises increased and I was being transfused more often than I should have been. But one day, through faith and the help of my brother, Greg, I reconnected with Evelyn and I began to get my health back on track.

Greg and his fraternity were holding an event to raise money for the sickle cell cause, so one day he was doing some research to find someone connected with a sickle organization to be a sponsor. After extensive calling, he was directed to Evelyn. They ended up talking, and he got the OK he was looking for. After their conversation was over, Greg told her how I was doing, and she let him know that I could call her, so I could meet with her in the clinic.

From then on, I started going back to the clinic. And I was put on a medicine called hydroxyurea that would help keep down the number of times I had a crisis. (I talk more about hydroxyurea in chapter 16). After I'd been on the medicine and going to the clinic again for a couple of months, Evelyn noticed how well I was doing. She said she wanted me to talk to other adults with sickle cell.

"James," she said to me, "we have a lot of people with sickle cell who are not coping particularly well with it, and I think it would be helpful for them if they could see and talk to someone who is."

I was working, staying very positive about my health, and most important, I was not letting my health interfere with my life, so she thought I was a perfect candidate. I knew that I wanted to speak to others with sickle cell and help them cope better just like the guest speakers had done for me in those support meetings when I was younger, so I jumped on the opportunity.

We sat in the clinic one day during my appointment, brainstorming and thinking how we could make it happen, but it never did. Even though I wanted to, and I seemed ready on the surface, in all fairness, on the inside I wasn't fully coping with the issue of having sickle cell all that well, either. I had not come to grips with the illness yet, so deep down I didn't think I was in a position to tell anyone else how they should cope. Everything was good health-wise, but emotionally I was torn, and in the end I never spoke. Now that I have come full circle and have accepted my illness, I have welcomed the chance to speak to other adults with sickle cell.

# CHAPTER 5

# <u>A CRISIS</u>

Having pain (called a crisis) is just another symptom of sickle cell. In fact, the pain is the single most recognized symptom associated with sickle cell, and it can range from mild to severe. The difference between the two is that while mild pain can be treated at home with painkillers like Percocet, the severe pain will result in a trip to the emergency for stronger medicine like Morphine or Dilaudid.

When I go to the emergency room or see my doctor, my pain is measured on a pain chart from one to ten. But to me the pain chart doesn't do it justice, because more often than not when I'm in the emergency room for pain, it feels a lot worse than a ten. When it comes to having a pain crisis, the famous question that everyone wants to know is, "What does the pain feel like?" It seems like such an easy question to answer, but it is the most difficult question for me. It's very difficult to describe my pain, to put it into words, so that you can get a full understanding of how it feels to me. I can say that the pain from a crisis is definitely one of the worst types of pain anyone can endure, and it usually can't be compared to any other pain I've experienced in my life.

To give you an example, when I was thirteen years old, I was racing my bike with a friend downhill at a local playground when I suddenly lost control and couldn't slow down. Before I knew it, I was careening down the hill so fast that I went straight into a cement wall. To brace myself and try to lessen the impact, I stuck my foot out and ended up breaking my big toe in the process. The initial pain I felt from breaking my big toe was less painful than what I normally feel during a crisis.

The pain from a crisis is such a chronic and debilitating pain that it can be very hard to cope with. The pain can get so severe that it is hard to do the most basic things, such as walking or lifting up a pitcher to pour a glass of water. Many times, I'm amazed at how I continue to go through these pains, but I know that nothing in life lasts forever, and the pain is only temporary.

Everyone with sickle cell may describe the pain of a crisis differently, but no matter how it's described, it's very serious. For me, the pain is a constant, throbbing, sharp, and penetrating pain that can be felt anywhere inside the body. Whenever I'm having a sharp pain in my back, chest, legs, hands, etc. it feels like someone is stabbing me with a butcher knife. Other times when my pain is throbbing, it feels as if someone has taken a hammer to my body, and is just pounding it against my skin repeatedly—like I'm a board, and they're just hammering away trying to break me in half. Sometimes it's a squeezing or penetrating pain. If I'm having it in my arms or legs, it literally feels like someone has put that part of my body in a vise grip and is twisting and tightening it, trying to cut off all my circulation on the inside. As I'm going through the pain, it feels like I can literally feel the cells inside my body trying to push through one by one. It's hard for me to talk because it hurts when I breathe.

When I am experiencing the pain of a crisis, I try to calm down, relax in a quiet place, and take slow deep breaths, hoping to ease the pain. The painful episodes usually strike in my back and my knees. If I'm having a sickle cell crisis in my back, I will grab at my back and just try to hold it so I feel no pain, but that doesn't help because the pain is deep inside my body. On the other hand, if the pain is in my knees, I will try to lie perfectly still with my knees either bent or as straight as possible, because it hurts me to move them. The pain in my back and knees gets so painful that it is hard for me to even get dressed to go to the emergency room. Growing up, it was trial and error for me trying to get rid of the pain. I tried everything from pain patches, to sitting in a bathtub filled with warm water, to using heating pads, but none of it worked. The best thing for me was to close my eyes and try to sleep.

Usually when I'm having a crisis, I know the spots where the pain can spiral out of control, so I waste no time in going to the hospital to be treated. When I turned eighteen, I had one of the worst sickle cell crises in my life, and I just remember being scrunched up on the bed screaming. It felt like someone was trying to kill me, and whoever it was had no regard for my body. The pain was so deep and penetrating in my back, it felt like a jackhammer was going through it, trying to break it up into a thousand little pieces. No matter how hard I tried, I could not even lie still. I was in the middle of the bed on my back with an IV in my arm, trying to grab ahold of anything because the pain was so uncontrollable. In my mind I was just thinking, "When is this going to end? Please somebody stop it!" I was violently grabbing at the guardrails on the bed as I scratched and pulled at the sheets in hopes of running away from the pain inside of me. The lines from my IV were swinging with every arm movements, and the nurses taking care of me that night were trying to keep their composure as they watched me.

I remember they kept yelling instructions to me over all the thrashing noise, telling me to be careful not to rip out my IV. Faintly I could hear the nurse saying, "We have called your doctor again. Tell me where it hurts."

"My back—it's in my back!" I kept screaming as my eyes were starting to swell up with tears. Between all of that, I would be saying to the nurses, "I need Morphine; give me Morphine!" I felt so helpless and miserable. I wished I could just fall asleep and make it all disappear.

I remember the doctor running in and out of my room repeatedly giving me the strongest doses of Morphine he could possible give me, but that did not help me even a little bit. He even left my room to call another doctor to ask how much of the medicine he could give me without it knocking me out stone cold. Every time he left my room, he came back in to give me more medicine through my IV.

Through all of this, I was screaming my lungs out on the sixth floor. I was so loud, I bet you could probably have heard me if you were standing on the first floor. It felt like with every dose of medicine I got, the pain in my back got worse. By the time it was over, it took a remarkable number of doses for my body to finally allow the medicine to overcome the significant pain that I had been suffering for the past few hours. I was finally spared and able to get some rest. However, it was an alarming situation for me because until that point my body had always taken to the medicine very well. But that night, it was like my body had flipped a switch and nothing worked to stop the pain. I was having the worst pain ever in my life, and I didn't know if I would ever have any relief. I can still visualize that moment in my mind, and I get chills from the thought of ever going through that experience again.

As a result of receiving so much Morphine that night, my respiratory and gastrointestinal systems began to slow down. I wasn't able to eat solid food, because I wouldn't be able to digest it. I had to be treated for this and wait days before I could eat again. In the meantime I was stuck on a liquid diet, only being able to eat things like ice cream, popsicles, applesauce, Jell-O, and chicken broth. Throughout the day, I would chew on ice cubes to satisfy my appetite. I also had to have a nasal tube inserted into my nose, which ran straight down through my throat and into my stomach to help me get the essential amount of nutrients I needed. I was even too weak to get up to go to the bathroom on my own, so I had to have a catheter inserted. If I did want to go to the bathroom, I would hit the nurse's call light button, and have to be assisted every step of the way. I felt helpless and miserable, because I was used to being able to do everything on my own. Even when I was in the hospital with an IV in my arm, I could usually still get around, but now this was impossible. My muscles were weak from me not using them, but every time I tried to use them, I was in so much pain. I literally wanted to just stay in bed, sleep, and not move an inch. During this sickle cell crisis, I was in the hospital for almost two weeks, but I learned something very important about myself and what a resilient mind can do for you.

Although I didn't realize it when I was going through that storm, resiliency was something that I had taught myself. My mind would be a tool that I would cultivate and use in every area of my life. By refusing to be broken down and shattered by this pain crisis and the aftermath of it, I learned I could get through anything I was faced with and make it out OK. After being immobile for almost a week, I got out of bed one day without the assistance of any nurses and made it to the bathroom on my own, even though I was still in incredible pain. Later on that night, I did something even more shocking that left my nurse flabbergasted. I told my nurse to stop the continuous flow of Morphine that I was still receiving through the IV from the PCA pump. (PCA stands for "patient-controlled analgesia." It's a pump that delivers medicine to a patient at a set time automatically.) I boldly told her, "Stop it. I don't need it." Just like that, I had decided to only call her for pain medicine when I needed it.

It didn't take much for a crisis to start. It could be triggered by the weather, stress, strenuous activity, infections, swimming in cold pools, or anything that caused a decrease of oxygen inside the body. A sickle cell crisis always brought an enormous amount of pain, but sometimes the pain was more violent than other times. Whenever I was going through these painful crises, the clock was my worst enemy because the pain just worsened with every minute that went by. A lot of times, my mind stayed fixed on the clock as I was going through a crisis. I would be at home, lying down in my bed with my bottle of painkillers on the nightstand, just waiting for the next time I could take them to control my pain. Each time I took them, I hoped that they would work right away; otherwise, it would be another miserable four hours for me, watching the hands on the clock. Although I hated taking the pills— because I hated the way it made my stomach feel groggy the next day, and I never wanted to become dependent on them—I had no choice when my pain was through the roof, and I was going through a crisis.

# CHAPTER 6

# <u>WAITING IN PAIN</u>

The darkest moment in my battle against sickle cell came when I was twenty-three years old. That was the first time I asked myself the question, "Why me?" Before, I had just accepted the hand that I was dealt and tried to make the most of my circumstances. What made that night different from any other night was not the fact that I was having another severe pain episode all over my body and could barely move. No, it was that I was ignored by emergency room medical staff and forced to wait for almost four hours in a chair, in pain, just to be seen. And the whole time, the emergency room staff treated me foully and showed me no mercy at all. This was an emergency room visit I quickly wanted to erase from memory, and prayed that I would never have to go through this kind of situation again.

I remember driving myself to the hospital that night and checking in at the front desk of the emergency room. When I got there, I was in so much pain that it was extremely hard for me to breath, and when I talked my voice crackled like an old chain-smoker. I was not getting enough air into my lungs, because my body was tensed up from the pain, and the pain made it hard for me to concentrate on breathing. After waiting an hour, I got up and went to the nurses' desk. She explained to me that they were still calling people back. I went back to my chair sat down. Another hour elapsed, and still there was no word on when I would be seen. I would repeatedly get up and go to the nurses' station to ask when I was going to be seen by a doctor, and they would just repeat to me vaguely, "We have your charts and we will get to you." What made the situation even worse is that a sickle cell patient is supposed to be considered urgent, so whenever I go to the emergency room I am supposed to be moved ahead of anyone with a less serious health issue. But that night, I could hear name after name being called, but no mention of mine.

It was very disturbing, and I wanted to just stand on top of the nurses' desk and yell at the top of my lungs, "I have sickle cell, and I'm in a lot of pain! I need to see a doctor now!" Of course, I did not. I just waited for a nurse to come get me and take me back, so I could be seen. I know emergency rooms can get a little crowded, but this was nothing out of the ordinary, yet it was beginning to be the longest wait time by far. I remember just trying to sit calmly in my chair until I heard my name being called, but it was a struggle for me. I kept shifting my body in my chair every five minutes as I occasionally put my head in my lap while repositioning myself so that I could not feel the pain I was in. But nothing worked to calm it. More time went by, and I decided to get up again to check on my name, but it was more of the same.

I was told, "We have your charts blah, blah, blah, and blah, blah, blah, we'll call you back when we can!" It was the same humdrum tune I had been hearing all night, and that's how it sounded to me at this point.

The last time I got up to check on my name, I was stopped in my tracks by the security guard working the lobby area; he wouldn't let me go to the nurses' station this time. The security guard was a round, oversized man with a protruding gut and a suffocating presence.

As he cut me off, he said to me, "Can I help you?"

"Yes, I need to see a doctor," I told him.

He asked, "Is this an emergency?"

I gave him a frustrated, "Yea." After all, it was the *emergency room.*

He then reached in his shirt pocket, and took out a pen and a Post-it note. He said, "Well, write your name down on this piece of paper, and have a seat. I will go check on it for you." Then he left with the piece of paper I had scribbled my name on. Five minutes later he came back and said to me, "The nurses told me they have already spoken with you, and they will get to you as soon as they can, so just have a seat and be patient."

Be patient? I thought to myself, I have been patient long enough already, and I can't take this shit anymore. Nevertheless, I ended up going back to my chair with my blood boiling and sat down for a minute. Then I looked at the clock again and realized how long I had been waiting. I finally I said to myself, "I've had enough of this shit! I'm done waiting; fuck it—I'm leaving now!" Finally, after waiting for almost four hours, I decided to get up and leave, because it was too much for me to handle. I stormed out of the emergency room violently, like a tornado ripping through a city. I left the emergency room, still in severe pain, but I couldn't put up with the pain of waiting anymore, so I made it to my car and headed home.

As soon as I got home, I unlocked the door and walked inside the house. My mother was standing in the kitchen with a perplexed look on her face. Before I could even get a word out, she said to me, "What happened? I thought you were going to the hospital." She clearly could see the distress on my face and the pain I was in.

I replied, "I did, but they would not *fucking see me!*"

"What?" she practically screeched, standing firmly in one spot, waiting for more details.

But I was in no hurry to talk, so I rushed straight to my room. In a rage, I twisted the door knob and flung it wide open like a mad man.

"I hate this! I hate this shit! Why me?" I screamed, grabbing the pile of books and things that were on my bed and tossing everything into the air. When they hit the ceiling fan it stopped momentarily, then everything crashed down to the floor. And I lost it, tears begin rolling down my face.

As my mother heard all this commotion going on, she darted into my room and said, "James, calm down and stop talking like that." Then she told me to gather my things, and said, "I'm going back to the emergency room with you." In less than five minutes flat, we stampeded back out the door like two wild buffalos, and I drove back over to the emergency room with her. When I got there, I signed back in and waited to be seen again. Only this time, I didn't have to wait forever. After a short while, I was finally seen by a doctor and, not surprisingly, I had to be hospitalized. That night was one of the lowest points in my life when it came to dealing with my sickle cell. It made me not want to face another day with this illness, and I had a lot of crazy thoughts running through my head. I just wanted to give up and throw in the towel, but I knew that I was stronger than my sickle cell, and no one or nothing was going to break me.

My mother was always with me when I went to the emergency room until I was about eighteen years old. That's when I decided that I wanted to take sole responsibility and become more independent about dealing with my sickle cell. I would go to the emergency room by myself and let her know if they were going to keep me overnight or if I was getting released. Up until this point, she had spent her entire time sitting in the emergency room with me, so I did not want to have her sit through the long hours of waiting for the different test results and things anymore. I appreciated everything she had done for me, and I wanted to give her a little break so she could focus on other things at home, like my siblings and, most important, rest. I had a phone in my room, so whenever I knew the plan for my treatment, I could just give her a call and let her know the details. My mother was a rock I could lean on—a very strong woman who was always there for me when I needed her to be. When I didn't feel like talking or was down from the medicine I was taking, she was there to take over for me.

When I was younger and we would go to the emergency room, my mother would usually be the one speaking directly to the doctors about which medicines I was on, and what medicines I had taken for pain. She would also help me remember the last time I was transfused and admitted to the hospital, so the nurses could chart all this information for the doctor. There was so much to remember, I can't begin to explain how she kept up with it all, because I sure couldn't. My turn to talk came when the nurse asked me about the pain I was having or when the doctor came into the room. I would have to open my mouth and speak to the doctor about when the pain started and where it was located in my body. I would also let the doctor know the amount of pain I was having. Nobody else could relay that information but me. At every opportunity she got, my mother was always teaching me life lessons on how to handle myself in the realm of health and in the outside world. A teacher in her own right, she used moments like this as her classroom to teach me about life. Every trip we made to the emergency room, she would remind me about the importance of remembering what medicines I was on, and what the doses were.

"James, you need to know this in case I am not around or able to come with you," she would say. She stayed persistent in telling me to ask the doctors and nurses what kinds of medicines they were giving me and why. "For your own sake, it is crucial for you to know what is going inside your body in case you have a reaction to it, so you know not to take it next time, or whatever the case may be."

The only time she would leave the emergency room was when it was time for me to get an IV put in my arm. She could not tolerate being in the room because the nurses always had trouble getting an IV in my arm. Occasionally, she would try to stick it out and stay in the room, but it was very hard for her. She would turn her head to the side and look the other way while they were trying to get the needle in my vein. They would try once, no luck—twice, still no luck. Cringing after the second time, she would leave the room and take a long walk down the hall, only to check back minutes later and see if they had got an IV started in my arm or hand before she came back to stay permanently. My mother always told me that watching me get stuck by those needles made her flesh crawl. But other than that, she was a real trouper.

When you have sickle cell, going to the emergency room can be its own beast. It's not unusual to be waiting lengthy times in the emergency room as a sickle cell patient. It was very much the norm and one of the disadvantages to having to be treated in the emergency room.

Sickle cell is always a guessing game for how severe the pain is going to be. A lot of times, I try to stay at home first. I take my medicines and drink my fluids to see if I can ride out the pain before I decide to go get looked at for my crisis. I don't want to make that trip out to the hospital, but I know it's inevitable when I have tried everything, and nothing is working—then that is my only option. Unfortunately the emergency rooms are something I have to rely on to be treated, so I have learned to deal with them. Sometimes it might take two or three days of me constantly repeating the pain medication cycle at home before I say, "OK, now I cannot tolerate the pain any longer. I have to go in."

CHAPTER 7

# <u>**NO RELIEF**</u>

Imagine going to the emergency room in pain and being accused by doctors and nurses who say that you are only there seeking the IV pain medications and that the severity of your pain is not as serious as you claim it to be. How would that make you feel? Furious, right?

When we go to the emergency room, we all expect the best treatment and care while we are there being nursed back to health. But when it comes to getting treated with narcotic painkillers, people with sickle cell have been given a bad rap. We have been negatively stereotyped and called "drug seekers" only looking for a quick fix. Instead of being treated for our condition, we are being judged by the doctors and nurses we depend on.

If you ask anyone with sickle cell if this sounds familiar, I will guarantee you that the answer to that question is, "Yes." Because at some point in our lives, any of us may have been faced with the stigma of being thought of as a "drug seeker." When that happens, it's like a ton of bricks falling on you. It just crushes you, and it is devastating to your morale. On top of all the pain and suffering that you are going through emotionally and physically, now you have medical professionals questioning your reasons for being in the hospital emergency room. There is no bright side to look at or words to express how you feel. As a young adult, when I was faced with this predicament, all I could do was ask myself, "Why? What makes me deserve this?"

As I recall it today, it was probably the worst experience I have had yet as a patient in the emergency room. I was already dressed in my hospital gown as I waited for the doctor to come into my room to see me. It was a hot summer night; the Wisconsin humidity had brought on another crisis and put me in an extreme amount of pain. On a scale from one to ten, it felt like a twenty-five, and it felt like it wasn't going away any time soon. As I lay on the hospital bed, I couldn't keep still. I was in so much pain that the tears were hard to keep suppressed, and there was nothing much I could do to keep them from falling silently down my cheeks. One by one, the tears kept dripping onto my hospital gown like water leaking from a broken faucet. I was in need of much attention, and I was making a lot of moaning noises. My room was right across from the nurse's station, so I had a perfect view of all the nurses in action. My moaning got the attention of one of the nurses at the nurses' station. I was expecting him to bring aid to me with IV fluids and pain medicine prescribed by the doctor. What I got, much to my dismay, was an agitated nurse who flew straight through my door like a bat straight out of hell! The nurse stormed hectically into my room and shouted at me to keep it down.

With a perplexed look on my face, I said in an

aggravated tone, "Well, how long before the doctor will be in? Because I'm in a lot of pain and no one has been in my room."

The reply I got back from the nurse was a quick, "Soon." And he left my room as quickly as he had entered it.

As the time continued to go by, I continued to moan and make noise from the intense pain I was having. Hearing the sounds echoing from out of my room, the nurse got up out of his chair behind the nurses' desk and came back into my room. Before I could even blink twice, he slammed the sliding glass door shut to my room and drew all the curtains closed so he couldn't see me.

I was totally shocked and very pissed off. I had been closed off from the rest of the hospital and left alone, so it was like I was not even there. Much to his satisfaction, I was out of sight and out of mind. I couldn't be seen or heard, and any time I pushed the call light, it was ignored until the doctor finally walked into my room to check me out and start my orders.

As soon I saw the doctor walk through my door, I wanted to scream, "Yes!" because I was so relieved. "Finally I can get some relief for my pain," I thought to myself. Once he came in the room, it only took about a minute for the doctor to assess me. He peered over his glasses and said, "OK, I will order you some morphine for your pain, and the nurse will be in shortly to give it to you."

As the doctor left my room to put the order in, I stared at the television on the wall to make the time go quicker as I waited for the nurse to return to my room with my pain medicine. Then I heard his drill sergeant voice saying, "I have your medicine right here. This should help you calm down. Which thigh would you like it in?"

I thought, "Wait a minute, they are not giving me an IV with fluids, and they did not draw my labs to check my blood counts either? This can't be right; they must have me confused with someone else."

For as long as I have been going to the emergency room for pain crises, never once have I been given pain medicine through an injection. Normally I get an IV with fluids, an oxygen tube in my nose, and pain medicine through the IV. By getting IV fluids, my body becomes more hydrated, which helps keep more red blood cells from sickling—the sickling is what causes the excruciating pain. This makes a big difference because medicine through an injection tends to get to the muscle quicker, but it is less effective because the dosage is lower. Since I was young, I have been given high dosages of medicine, so I have built a higher tolerance to the medicines. The injection, to me, would be the equivalent of taking an over-the-counter Tylenol. Most people do not understand that the amount of pain medicine sickle cell patients need exceeds what the average person could handle by a long shot. Aside from all that, there was no mention of drawing blood for lab work. Lab work was very important, because it could indicate how much sickling my red blood cells were going through.

Minutes after receiving the pain medicine, I was still in tremendous pain and making a lot of noise. Suddenly, the nurse darted back into the room and said, "Stop making all this damn noise in here! You are not in that much pain; I gave you medicine already!"

Man, I couldn't believe what I was hearing. Right away, I wanted to say, "Today is not the day for this kind of harassment. I am already in enough pain." But I refrained from doing so to avoid a confrontation.

Then the nurse said, "This pain is not killing you! If you were in that much pain you would have come in earlier!"

I felt so slighted and taken aback by the nurse's ludicrous comment that I responded with hostility. I said, "I am in pain. You don't know how it feels, so shut the hell up!"

He stared back at me coldly and asked me in a loud tone, "Do you want to leave?"

"No," I said. "I came here to be treated!" I couldn't believe this was happening to me, and to be treated like this was a total disgrace.

As the tension in the room lingered, I asked to speak to the doctor, and the nurse exited the room immediately. A couple of minutes later there was no sign of the doctor, but the nurse returned in a milder manner. He said, "The doctor ordered another dose of morphine for you and that's it!"

So while I was being administered my last Morphine injection, I was also being handed my discharge papers and told to follow the instructions as it related to my emergency room visit.

Nothing had been resolved. My pain was still there. I had been forced to wait a long time for my pain medicine, and the dosages the nurse gave me were inadequate. When I go to the emergency room, I know I am dealing with a host of different doctors and nurses, who must use their own judgment and speculate on whether a patient is indeed in enough pain to require large amounts of pain medications. I understand that emergency rooms may deal with "drug seekers" on some level; when it comes to sickle cell patients there needs to be different standards set in place even though we have frequent hospital visits and require high dosages of pain medicine. What I have observed is when I am alone in the emergency room it becomes more difficult to receive the adequate treatment that is needed to reduce my pain level and increase my comfort level. The first thoughts that pop into my head every time I'm forced to go to the emergency room are, "I hope that they will see me right away" and "How will the doctors and nurses treat me? Will they take their time so they can do the right assessment of my pain so they can prescribe the right amount of medication and tests if they need to? Or will they go based off of preconceived notions that they may have of sickle cell patients?" I also have to wonder, "Will they possibly be thinking I am putting on a front, and my pain is not as bad as I describe it to be?" Who knows? But even though I might have these concerns, I do not let them overtake me. Instead, I choose to remain optimistic with a positive outlook, and carry on like the soldier that I am. And like a soldier in combat boots ready to do battle, I am prepared to face whatever comes my way.

When it comes to relaying my pain to doctors, nurses, friends, bosses, or whomever, the main thing I want people to know and understand is that the pain is indeed very real. The harsh reality of having sickle cell is that we deal with constant pain on a daily, weekly, monthly, and yearly basis, and it affects every area of our lives.

Fortunately for me, I have been able to maintain a balanced lifestyle while controlling and managing my sickle cell. However, other people who have the same condition are not so lucky. No one knows for sure the amount of pain a crisis may bring or how it will affect us because, like fingerprints, we are not identical. We each have a different genetic makeup, so the most effective action is to take precautions to try to prevent pain.

Regardless of how much you try to prevent it, eventually the pain will come—it is not something that you can pick and choose, when you have it and when you don't. We have to accept that as a fact. Sometimes pain can be triggered suddenly and other times the pain is already there, but then intensifies. One minute you can go from laughing, joking, and having a good time, to the next minute, ailing and feeling miserable. Many times when I was younger, whenever I went swimming, I would have an immediate crisis once I got out of the water. It was something about the cold water that triggered my body into a crisis. Other times, it was caused by not drinking enough fluids. In general, when it comes to having a sickle cell crisis, there are no exaggerations for the pain I feel or have. One thing that is even more demoralizing than the pain itself, though, is having people doubt you when you say that you are in pain.

·

# CHAPTER 8

## <u>A MOTHER'S LOVE</u>

**M**y mother is a very strong individual; when it came to my illness she was even stronger than I was. She was the anchor that kept me grounded, and she always stayed so positive. Anytime I was down or having a rough day, she always tried to get me to look at the bright side of things. And every time I went through a crisis, she felt the pain just as much as I did, but never once did she let me see her sweat or drip a tear. And when it came to me and all my stays in the hospital, she was by my side every step of the way and the best support I could ever have asked for. Whenever I was going to the doctor for my checkups, she was there. Whenever I needed to be taken to the emergency room because of the sickle cell pain I was going through, she was there, always offering her kind words and loving touch. Whenever I needed to pick up my prescriptions, she was there to take me. Whenever I needed to be admitted to the hospital and stay for an extended period of time, she would spend her entire time there. When it was time for her to go to sleep, she would make a bed out of the leather reclining chair that was in the corner next to my bed. In the middle of the night, I would wake up and glance over from time to time and see her, with the covers that the nurse had handed her all drawn across her body. Looking at her through the guardrails on my bed, I knew she didn't get the best sleep, but she tried to get as comfortable as possible and never complained about it. On days when she wasn't able to spend the night with me, she would stay from the morning until visiting hours were over, and I would still be saddened by her leaving. She meant the world to me, and whenever she was there, I always felt better.

Even though my pain was bad enough, I could not imagine how it must have felt to be in my mother's shoes and what it must have meant for her to see her baby boy with IVs in his arm, in so much pain. Anytime I went through a crisis, it left my whole body aching awfully, and there wasn't a thing she could do for me to relieve that pain. I know she must have felt so helpless, and if she could have taken all of my pain away and put it all on herself, she would have done it at the drop of a hat. She was that kind of woman. I remember when I was young and we didn't have much food in the cabinets, before she would even think about fixing herself a meal, she would always make sure everyone in the house had eaten first. My mother always took the time to think about everyone else before she spent a moment on herself. At times, I felt a sense of guilt because I know all of her attention had to be focused on me because of my health. That's why every chance I got, I always thought about ways to repay her. I knew she hated seeing me sick just as much as I hated being sick, so I wanted to put off going to the hospital as much as possible to show her and my family just how tough I was. After visiting me in the hospital, every time she left my bedside she would kiss me on my forehead and say, "I love you," and then look me in the eyes and say, "Now get some rest,

James. I'll see you in the morning." Sure enough, the next day, as my mother had promised me, she would be there right about the same time I had finished eating my breakfast.

Reflecting back on it now, I know it must have taken a toll on her, but she never expressed it once. Even in the most difficult of times, when I would be crying my eyes out with tears pouring down my face, she just tried her hardest to make sure I was comfortable and happy in many different ways—like bringing my favorite toys from home, or stopping at the store to pick up my favorite snacks, or just having the nurse's aide change the sheets on my bed and get me some new pillows. She did it all to please me, while I dealt with the pain. That's why I can say she's the best mother in the whole world, and I love her whole-heartedly.

Thinking back to when I was younger, about ten years old, I remember sitting at the kitchen table and my mother asking me what I wanted to be when I grew up. I would always tell her that I wanted to be a professional football player in the NFL. I loved the game of football, and I would play it every weekend with my brother, Greg, and some close friends from our neighborhood. I always pretended that I was Dion Sanders wearing a number twenty-one jersey, and I tried my best to imitate his moves. Any time I caught a touchdown or made an interception, I would do a little dance and high step in the end zone, just like him. He was my favorite player of all time—because of him twenty-one is still my favorite number. While my mother listened to me speak about football passionately, she would always try to steer me toward other jobs, because she knew realistically it was not physically possible for anyone with sickle cell to play contact sports at a high level. She would say to me, "James, find a skill using your hands, something that would be less stressful on your body and more realistic for you to do."

Over time, she tried to get me interested in playing the drums by taking me to different music stores and trying to convince me to give it a shot to see if I liked it. She would say to me, "You know, your Uncle Mark plays instruments. He's really good at it. He taught himself to play and he loves it." My mother also suggested art as a way for me to make a career, and she would randomly go to the store and pick up sketch pads for me along with other art supplies. However, I never tried my best. I was too much in love with football. It was etched in my mind like a memory, and I did not want to think about anything else.

The best time for my family was at the kitchen table. We spent a lot of quality time there. My brother, my sisters, and I would sit at the kitchen table talking, laughing, and joking around while we ate our meals. Whichever parent cooked the meal would stay in the kitchen with us until all the food was served, and then go in the other room. My parents ate their meals together in a different room, but close enough to where they could still kept an eye on us. Some mornings, when I was in pain from a crisis, I would sit at the kitchen table in the chair with my feet on the seat and my body balled up in a knot. I felt like it would help to position my body this way and not move. That was the only way for me to try to deal with the pain I was in, if I had not taken medicine or it was not working. Greg would sit at the opposite end of the table screaming at me to put my feet down because he thought I was goofing off. My mom or dad would come running in the kitchen and ask me why I was not sitting in the chair right, and that's when I would tell them I was hurting. At times, no one in my family really knew how much pain I was in or when I was starting to have pain if I didn't tell them or was not crying and moaning. Seeing me jaundiced was a normal thing for them. Nevertheless, they all knew my pain was real, and each of my siblings played a significant part in looking after me when the pain came on. That's how we were raised by my parents: love your family and take care of your family. We were a tight knit group.

As you can tell by now, my mother has played an integral role in my life in helping me get through all my battles with sickle cell, and she never let on to me how much it affected her life. She was so even-keeled and such a dedicated mother and great mom in making sure all of her children did their best to succeed, including me. Her top priority was always making sure I was happy, and she would never put herself before any one of us. I speak a lot about my mother when it comes to my life with sickle cell because she has been such a dedicated parent, by my side every step of the way, and it's very easy for me to say that she has done a lot for me in making sure I got the best possible treatment as a kid—and even as an adult.

Today, I still call my mother, just like I did when I was younger, because I know she still worries about me and wants to know what's going on with me, from my appointments to the type of medicine and treatment I am getting. Even though I handle it all on my own now, I think that her wanting to be there for me will never go away because she has been there for me my entire life. I know, at times, it may have been a burden or difficult to handle, but she never spoke one word to me or anyone else about it, and I am truly blessed by her presence in my life. There are not enough words to express the love I have for her, because she has no doubt shouldered a heavy load. Her presence around me when I was sick helped me develop a strong emotional connection with her. My mother has always been there for me emotionally. She's the one I can talk to about anything, and she always seems to understand me and know where I'm coming from. When I have nothing to say, she knows how I feel just by the look on my face, and that's important for me.

My dad has also been there for me. He was my first hero and the first person that I looked up to. Everyone always told me I looked just like him. Once I got older, I remember hearing stories about him boasting to people he knew that I would be born on his birthday, but I came two days later.

My dad was always there, so he took his opportunities early on to instill qualities in me to get me through life when it came to my illness. He told me to never accept it as a weakness and to use it to my advantage. With that came a lot of tough love, because he never felt the need to treat me any different. If I fell, he would be the one to tell me to get back up, dust myself off, and keep going. If I got caught doing something I wasn't supposed to be doing, he would discipline me.

I even remember him, one muggy summer day while everyone else was gone, teaching my cousin Perry and me how to box in the living room. Like a professional boxing instructor, he would yell out, "Right-left-right, again, right-left-right!" to my cousin and me as we both smirked and took our turns hitting the target—my dad's two hands outstretched in front of his chest. I think that, as an army veteran, he wanted me to be just as tough as he was if not tougher, and I think that when it came to seeing me in the hospital it was hard for him. I believe that's why he didn't visit me as much as I would have liked. Strangely enough, I can picture him with his stomach in knots and burning up inside when he came to visit. But whenever he did come to the hospital, I was all smiles, and we had a pleasant time.

My dad has instilled so many values in me and shown me how to be a provider for my own future family when that time comes. I could never discredit what he has done. Every day, I would watch him go to work so he could provide for our family, and he always worked hard at it. His favorite thing to tell me was that I needed to work harder and smarter, and there would be plenty of opportunities for me. I have always taken that to heart, and every day I continue to use knowledge he has taught me.

# CHAPTER 9

# **HOSPITALS**

$S$ickle cell is a blood disorder where the red blood cells in your body lose oxygen, which causes the red blood cells to begin to change form from their natural disc shape to a sickle (or as I think of it, banana) shape. Because of their curved shape, the sickle red blood cells begin to stick against the walls of your veins, causing a blockage that prevents all the other red blood cells from passing through and delivering the proper amount of oxygen to your body. When the red blood cells can't deliver the adequate amount of oxygen to the body tissues and organs, the body goes into a crisis, experiencing an excruciating amount of pain. The pain can be felt be in your arms, legs, back, head, chest, and joints. It's wherever the blood flows. When organs are deprived of oxygen the consequences can be serious and even fatal. The only way for me to get rid of a pain crisis is with the use of strong narcotic pain killers like oxycodone, Percocet, Vicodin, and Morphine as well as fluids and rest.

Another important part of my treatment is fluids. Water contains oxygen, so by continually increasing the amount of water I'm taking in, the red blood cells get more of the oxygen they need. Water also acts as a lubricant to push the sickle cells through the veins. The amount of fluids someone with sickle cell should be drinking to stay sufficiently hydrated is approximately eight to twelve cups a day. By the time I reached twelve years old, I learned how to tell if I was getting enough fluids in my body by checking the color of my urine. I knew if it was dark yellow or orange looking, like the color of apple juice, I wasn't getting enough fluids and I needed to drink more. On the flip side, if my urine looked clear, like water, than I was getting the right amount of fluids to keep my body hydrated properly. When I was younger and going through a crisis at home, I would try to drink as much water as I possibly could to eliminate the pain I was in. Every five minutes I would be filling my cup and drinking one cup after another, trying to guzzle gallons of water like a fish so that my crisis would pass. I would take in so much water that it made my belly stick out and I would be going to the bathroom nonstop. While I was in the hospital one day, a nurse made a comment to me about my stomach saying it looked like a pregnant woman's belly. From that day forward, it became a running joke between us every time I saw her. Drinking enough water, resting, and taking the pain medicines were the steps I needed to take if I wanted to make it through a crisis at home. But if the painkillers and extra fluids didn't help, my next and only option would be to take a trip to the hospital. It was a place that I was all too familiar with, and I dreaded going.

Once I arrive at the emergency room, the routine is always the same.

**Step One—Vital Signs:** The nurse will take all my

vital signs to see if there is anything else to be concerned about. First, a blood pressure cuff is placed around my arm. Because I'm in pain, my blood pressure may have a tendency to be higher, since the heart is working harder to deliver the blood. Next, my temperature is taken to see if I have a fever. A fever can trigger a crisis, or it can indicate that something more is going on, like pneumonia or some kind of infection. Even when I am not having a sickle cell crisis, if I have a temperature of one hundred or higher, I'm advised to go straight to the hospital. No ifs, ands, or buts. Because there could definitely be something going on that I'm unaware of, and left unchecked it could potentially lead to something quite serious. Last, a little device called a pulse oximeter (pulse ox for short) is placed on the tip of my finger to check my oxygen level. This device doesn't hurt; it opens up like a clothespin and goes on the tip of the index or middle finger. The pulse ox shows a number between zero and one hundred, which indicates my saturated level of oxygen being carried in the blood through the. A good number would be ninety-four or higher, which means my lungs are getting an adequate amount of oxygen flowing through them and are functioning well. However, if the number is too low, I will have to be placed on oxygen. I am often placed on oxygen as a precaution, because it aids in the treatment of a crisis by reducing the chances of more sickling.

**Step Two—Pain Assessment:** The nurse will begin to assess my pain by asking me where I feel it, and to rate the pain on a scale from one to ten. There are so many places where pain can occur that can lead to serious infections or cause damage to organs that it is very important to identify the source of my pain so that the medical staff can perform the necessary tests.

After the pain is evaluated, the doctor will come

into my room and order some tests. The first (of possibly many) is a blood test called a CBC (complete blood count). This blood test is important because the doctor can check to see what my hemoglobin levels and white blood cell counts are. It's best if the white blood count is low and the hemoglobin is not. White blood cells fight infections, so any elevation of the white blood cells could indicate some type of infection. Hemoglobin is the protein in the red blood cells that carries oxygen to all parts of the body and gives them their red color. A person with sickle cell will usually have a lower hemoglobin level than someone without it. It's very important that my level doesn't get too low because that may require me to have a blood transfusion. My normal hemoglobin level is around nine but it can vary from person to person. The lower my hemoglobin levels get, the worse the crisis will be. While the blood tests are being sent out, the doctor may also choose to order a urine sample just to make sure my liver and kidneys are functioning well, and there are no signs of infection going on with them.

**Step Three—Pain Relief:** In the final step, the nurse will provide me with immediate pain relief, which begins with putting an IV in my arm. Without an IV, nothing else can be done to help relieve the pain. Receiving IVs is probably the worst thing of the night! They bring a lot of pain and frustration since they are so difficult to start on me. Because people with sickle cell usually have smaller veins and become easily dehydrated, the veins will have a tendency to move and roll, so the nurses are not always able to find an adequate vein for the IV. Also, over time veins develop scar tissue from being repeatedly poked and can't be used, so I find myself constantly being stuck by a needle. At times, it seems like I've been cursed, because not only do I have a chronic illness where I have to have my blood drawn often and IVs put in me, I was also given veins that make it even more difficult. I have gotten poked by needles so many times that IVs are now getting harder by the day. I have even had to have IVs placed in my neck and chest. The IV is essential for people going through a crisis, because it gets them the proper fluids they need to help the body rehydrate, so the red blood cells can pass through the body more easily. This is also where the medicine will be given to provide the pain relief.

Once the IV is finally started and the fluids are going, it's time for me to receive pain medicine. That could be Dilaudid, Morphine, or Demerol, depending on what the doctor orders. The second the pain medicine goes in through the IV, I know right away because I can feel it in the pit of my stomach. It provides me with such relief and keeps me calm for the time being. In an instant, I go from being in intense pain and not wanting to move to being able to relax a little and not feel the constant stabbing or throbbing from the pain. It's good to be able to feel my pain ease a bit, because the pain I go through is the type that could make the world's strongest man look feeble. But sometimes, the medicine does not work right away, which means they have to give me more and more until it finally kicks in. If the pain is still there and at a level where I am not comfortable, I know I'm going to have to be admitted to the hospital and stay overnight.

I have spent so much of my life in and out of the hospital that I have considered it my second home. From the time I was born until now as an adult, hospitals have been a major part of my life. I can't think of a year when I didn't spend at least a day overnight in the hospital. To this day, I'm still being admitted to the hospital when I have a severe crisis. I can spend anywhere from one night to a week or more; it just depends on how fast the pain can be controlled, and if there is anything else going on. Spending nights in the hospital will never cease for me because it is a part of my life. At times, it has felt like I never left the hospital because I was back and forth so much that I never had time to miss them. It was a cycle for me—I was in, then out, then back in again. But the longer I stayed out of the hospital, the more of a personal achievement it was for me. It's funny, because many people never spend more than a week in their entire lives in the hospital, but for many people with sickle cell a week can be normal for treating a crisis. As a kid, I did my best to make sure I treated it like home by bringing different toys to play with while I was there, and clothes and things to wear around the hospital to make my stay was comfortable as possible. A couple of times, I even went as far as hanging posters up on the door of my room. It gave my room its own personal feel, and everyone who walked into my room couldn't help but notice the new makeover.

From the age of eight, I was always admitted to St. Joseph's Hospital. Whether I checked in at admissions, or came up from the emergency room, I knew I was headed for the sixth floor. This was the children's floor, and it became very familiar to me. I was recognized by almost everyone who worked on that floor. From the moment I set foot on the floor, almost every single nurse would recognize me. I was very popular among the nurses, and it showed. The ones who took care of me the most would always make their presence felt and would get my attention by waving or smiling and saying, "Hi" to me as soon as I entered. Many of the staff who worked on that floor knew me on a first name basis—everyone from the nurses, to the nurse's aides, to the housekeeper, and sometimes all the way down to the staff in the kitchen. The girls who worked in the kitchen and brought the food trays up to my room would bring me extra cookies, snacks, or even the daily newspaper.

Even though everyone was always glad to see me, everyone (including myself) hated to see me have to come back to the hospital again. When it happened, many of the nurses would feel sorry for me and say things like, "Awe, back again," or "We told you we didn't want to see you in here again for a while."

I remember one particular nurse named Kathleen, not long before she retired, reminiscing about me and telling me stories of how she watched me grow right before her eyes from a little boy to a young man. She said she could not believe how fast the time flew by, and because I was in the hospital often she got to know me very well. Many times over the years, she would tell me how she thought of me like I was a part of her family and I was such a tough kid. Countless times before she left, I remember her saying to me, "It was just amazing for me to see you grow, and to know that I took care of you all those years was a joy."

## CHAPTER 10

# <u>GETTING IV'S</u>

When you have sickle cell, IVs comes with the territory. They are a key component in helping you get the necessary medicines, fluids, and antibiotics that you need. Sometimes they are also used to add contrast agent for CAT scans and MRIs.

When I was little and having a crisis, I used to dread going to the emergency room, because I knew that being stuck by a long sharp needle was inevitable, and the pain would be god-awful. The needles were not an easy thing for me to deal with, because the pain from the needles felt terrible. Sometimes it would leave my whole hand, wrist or arm bruised from all the digging, probing and poking in my skin. Unfortunately, I would have to endure being stuck multiple times for blood counts and the IVs used to treat my pain.

To prepare me for being stuck and to try to prevent the burning, pinching, hurting sensation of the needles, the nurses would rub numbing cream on the area where they were looking to insert the needle before they started. But nothing could stop the pain I felt from the needle going in through my skin and poking me. Many days and nights when I was a kid, I remember being taking into a cold room where they had a bunch of drawers stocked with different sizes of needles and a hard table covered only by a sheet as they tried to get an IV in me. My mother would be on one side of me and the two nurses on the other. While one nurse held me down and tried to put the IV in the other nurse would say to me in her soft delicate voice, "Hold still, honey, and squeeze my hand tight on the count of three." But as soon as I felt the needle I would be wiggling on the table, trying to free my arm. They tried every single little trick to distract me from what was going on around my arm, but I still would be squirming when I felt that needle.

A decade later, they were still having trouble putting IVs in. But nothing was scarier than the time I had to have an IV placed in my chest. Even the IV that had been placed in my neck on a rare occasion was not as bad as the ordeal I was about to go through. The nurses were having such a hard time getting an IV in the veins of my arms and hands that the last resort for me was to have one placed in my chest for a short term use. I was running a high fever, and I needed to get pain medicines, fluids, and antibiotics into my system quickly to control my fever and relieve all the torturous pain I was experiencing all over my body. Rarely did the nurses ever hit a vein with one needle stick; it always seemed to take at least two times for them to get an IV line in me, if I was lucky. The more times I got stuck by the needle the more I grew accustomed to how it felt and what it took to get one in. As a result, I had developed a weird obsession with watching them put the IV in. Everyone thought it was a little crazy because I would literally sit there and watch the entire process, and I would barely flinch or budge. A lot of times, the nurses starting the IVs would tell me to look away as I was about to feel the incision. But I didn't want to be shocked by the needle when it pierced my skin, so I watched intently, like a tiger staring down his prey. In my lifetime, I have had thousands of IVs put in but nothing could ever prepare for me for what happened on the night I had one placed in my chest.

On this particular night, I counted a total of five tries before the nurses finally gave up and flagged the doctor down to come into my room and decide another option for me. Everyone tried their hand at it to see if they would be the one to have any luck with my veins, but nothing. Out of all the attempts, no one was successful. All the different techniques were used, and I would get more stressed each time they didn't get it right. In one case, I had a hot pack put on my arms to make my veins warm so they would pop up on the surface and become more visible, but nothing. My veins continued to hide. Then I had a blood pressure cuff put on my arm, inflated to the max to hold the veins in the spot and make the veins rise, so when the nurses threaded the needle through my skin, it would go right into the vein. As my arm dangled loosely, it felt like a giant rubber band was squeezing my arm until it practically went numb, but still no luck. They tried an infrared light to see where the veins were hiding under the skin. As the nurse looked at my veins under the infrared light, I snuck a peek also. They looked like a bunch of zigzag lines. But this didn't work either.

By the third attempt, my arms were starting to feel like a pin cushion, and I was being stuck with one needle after another. Each nurse preferred to use a different size needle in my arms, but still had no luck with an IV. Not even a speck of blood would ooze out of the newly made holes. I could feel the needles under my skin just tugging, ripping, and digging into to my vein (or the place where my vein should have been) as the nurse continued to move the needle in and out—forward a little then back a little—trying to chase the vein, then taking it out and trying another spot, leaving my arm all bruised up from all the sticking. There was no use for any Band-Aids—if they were placed on me, they were just there as decoration because my veins would not give any blood.

They called in a nurse who specialized in putting IVs in babies and trauma patients to come into my room, but even she could not end this fiasco. The fever, along with my small veins and the dehydration, just made it too difficult for anyone to be successful. I knew that the nurses were also getting frustrated—maybe even more than I was, because they were scratching and pulling at their hair as they tried again and again and again.

A couple of times, I saw my nurse leave my room only to peek back in to see if an IV was started, and when there was another failed attempt she would have this look of doubt on her face. I was becoming more and more depressed because I needed some relief from everything. I was a little unsure of what was next, but I knew I needed an IV, and I wasn't going anywhere until I had one, even if that meant to keep trying.

I looked down and saw the thick veins bulging out of my legs and feet. I suggested to my nurse that she could put an IV in my leg or foot, but she shook her head and told me, "No." There were just too many potential complications for getting blood clots, with less circulation in the legs and feet, so they couldn't do it. I remember having an IV in my foot as a baby as I hobbled around the crib, looking over the rails at my mother, and father sitting in the chair while I spat out words, laughed, screamed, and entertained myself while I was in the hospital. But not this time. My lower extremities were off limits.

As a last resort, the doctor was called into my room by the nurse. He was this big guy, over six feet tall, with a bald head and must have weighed close to three hundred pounds. If you asked me, I would say that he could have played lineman on any given Sunday for some team in the NFL. But nevertheless he was a gentle giant—an emergency room doctor who had treated me before, so I felt secure that something would get done. Doctors don't usually put IVs in patients. All my life, never had one doctor came into the room and used any type of needle or syringe on me before. Not even a finger prick. That was not their job; that was a job for the phlebotomist, nurse, or someone else that specialized in starting IVs and drawing blood. But tonight was different.

It was the first time something like this had happened to me, and of course I was not at all delighted. The doctor said to me, "James, we need to get an IV in you now so that we can get you going on some fluids to stop your fever from going up any further, and to get you some relief for the pain that you are in." Then he asked, "Are you hanging in there?"

"Yes," I said.

"How's your pain, on a scale from one to ten?"

"A ten!"

"Well, don't worry. We will get you going on some pain meds as soon as we get an IV in you. As you can see, tonight the nurses are having trouble with your veins, and we can't keep sticking you, so I am going to have to put an IV in your chest."

I thought, "Oh great—an IV in my chest. Ouch." I

never have been one to complain about needles or be afraid of needles, but I think I had a slight panic attack when I heard those words. The fear of the unknown was driving me crazy as the doctor continued to speak to me about putting an IV in my chest.

He said, "There are some things I have to tell you. I am the only one who can perform this procedure on you, but there's some risk involved. There is a chance the needle could puncture your lung, and your lung could collapse if it goes in too far or I go at the wrong angle. Now I have put many of these in patients before, but I still have to let you know about the risk and what's going on."

As the doctor was explaining the procedure that was about to take place, an image of a balloon bursting as it was being stuck by a giant needle popped into mind. I feared if anything went wrong this is what would happen to my lung.

Then I became adamant about not having the IV placed in my chest. I went into a tirade, screaming at the doctor, "No, I don't want it!" I was drenched with the fear of thinking that if my lung collapsed I might possibly die in the emergency room all alone, and it made me sick to my stomach.

Now I needed a minute, because my mind was in shambles. I just wanted to hear my mother's voice and talk to her. I politely asked the doctor if I could make a phone call first. As the doctor tried to put me at ease, I remember him telling me, "When the nurses draw IVs in your arm, there are complications that could happen to you as well. Your veins could also collapse, or we could hit an artery or nerves."

Yeah, right. Was he trying to say the risk was the

same? I refused to acknowledge that it was the same at all. Finally, with some convincing and a moment to calm down, I was persuaded to let him do it.

He leaned over me as he jacked the bed up to its highest point, and then began to stick the needle in my chest. I felt pressure in my chest, as if I was drowning in of pool of my own sweat, partly due to my fever and more due to anxiety of what was happening. But I just laid as still as possible and prayed that everything would go smoothly. A blue curtain was placed above my chest to prevent me from seeing anything that was going on from my neck down. Two nurses held the curtain as they assisted the doctor. Even if I looked down, I could not see past this shield, so I had no idea of what was happening on the other side of it. It was like a surgical procedure without the anesthetic. It lasted about twenty minutes, with the doctor carefully sliding the long tube with the needle inside my chest inch by inch. As he maneuvered his instruments, I was praying and sweating as he twisted the long needle with his big hands like pliers.

He asked me, "Are you doing OK?"

I replied, "Yes."

Then he said, "You're doing great. We're almost done." There was one last push, and it was finally over. I thanked God that I made it through this painful and frightening ordeal. Now I could have my medicine, antibiotics, and fluids to start my recovery from the fever and pain.

# CHAPTER 11

# **PAIN MEDICINE**

The only thing I remember was nodding off and feeling relief from the medicine, and then I was sound asleep. I was so heavily sedated from the pain medicine in the emergency room that the doctor had to perform a sternum rub on me to be sure I was still responsive. The last thing I could picture was lying on the bed in that freezing examining room with warm blankets wrapped around me like I was a mummy. The warm blankets felt good around my body; they kept me from shivering because the emergency rooms were always so cold. A nurse explained that it was cold to prevent the spread of germs. After receiving a couple of doses of medicine and falling asleep, the next thing I knew was suddenly being woken up by a frantic nurse who kept yelling at me to breathe. I had been given Dilaudid for the pain, resulting in shallow breathing, falling oxygen levels, and a slowed heart rate.

Most of my pain crises tended to come at night or in the early morning; so many times I would get woken up out of my sleep because of the pain. It was something that I never understood, but it was something I was alert for and managed to cope with. My motto would always be, "If I could make it through the night, then everything would be just fine."

The nurse continued to call my name and say, "James, you need to breathe. Make sure that you continue to breathe. How's your pain doing? What is your pain level at now?" It was a barrage of questions from her as she did everything in her power to keep me awake and focused on breathing normally.

To make sure that my oxygen levels didn't drop too low, I had also been placed on two liters of oxygen. The use of oxygen during a sickle cell crisis was always a standard treatment for me, but this time it was needed because the medicine was really slowing my breathing down. As a precaution, sickle cell patients should be placed on oxygen when they come into the emergency room in a crisis. Anytime I'm going through a crisis, the red blood cells are turning from round to sickle-shaped because they are losing oxygen. Oxygen helps prevent more cells from sickling, so providing a steady flow of oxygen to the body helps in pain relief.

My response to the overflow of instructions being thrown at me like fastballs was a flustered, "OK, I am breathing," as I would lift my head up and open my eyes for a split second, and then drop my head back down to my pillow. I could not stay coherent for two seconds. The medicine was making me drowsy, but it was also beginning to ease the pain. I knew it had already kicked into my system and was already working; I could tell because it was definitely starting to put me to sleep. However, this was no different for me from any other time I was in the emergency room and receiving medicine. The one thing I did know, though, was if the medicine I received through the IV in the emergency room put me to sleep, this would be a short-lived crisis. However, if I needed dose after dose repeatedly without the medication putting me to sleep, I would be in for a long crisis. When it came down to it, I always wanted the medicine to put me to sleep because then I would not feel the intense pain anymore. But after the umpteenth time of being told to breathe by my nurse as I zoned in and out, I passed out for good, and when I woke up it was ten o'clock in the morning.

I woke up to a lady with an olive skin complexion and long black curly hair standing over me. Not recognizing her the first time, I did a double take before I figured it out it was my doctor, Dr. Jackson. She asked me, "How you are doing?"

I replied, "I'm fine." I was still groggy from the medicine and slowly waking up. It was a surprise to me because I did not expect to see her hovering over my hospital bed like a helicopter this early, so I gave her a puzzled look. I said, "I feel much better than I did last night. I'm still having pain, but it seems to be going down."

She said, "That's good," and went on to give me the rundown of the stats from the examination in the emergency room. The results list consisted of things like blood levels, liver counts, x-rays, and anything else that might have been checked from the previous night. After she read her list of results, she told me what the plan was for this hospital stay and how she was going to treat my pain so that I could get better and be released. That involved what pain medication I would be receiving, the dose that was prescribed, and how often I could call the nurse to have it delivered to me.

Her final question was, "Do you know that we had

to perform a sternum rub on you?"

Guessing it was not good, I asked, "What is a sternum rub?"

"Good question," she said, going on to explain in a way that was easy for me to understand that a sternum rub is a way for doctors, nurses, or paramedics, to check how responsive a person is, to see if the person is conscious. One way to do this is by making a fist and sliding it up and down the person's sternum with a good amount of pressure. It can be awfully painful and even cause bruises, but from my level of consciousness (or should I say unconsciousness), I didn't feel a thing.

I was thinking, "Wow! I must have really been out of it this time."

After Dr. Jackson finished talking, the room grew silent for a minute, like it had just been sucked out by a vacuum. As she left the room, she said, "I will be back tomorrow to follow up on you and assess how you are doing." Then she walked away, until I could no longer hear the sounds of her heels clicking against the floor with each stride.

Never once had it occurred to me that I might have been in any trouble or that anything bad could happen to me from the pain medicine I was given in the hospital. I just relied on it to relieve my pain crisis and never really thought too deeply about the outcomes and side effects of taking the medication while in the hospital. I do know that prolonged use of medication has its long-term effects on the body and organs, but never once did I consider the thought of having too much medication in me, that it just knocks me out.

During my hospital stays, my mother would always

find a time to quietly exit the room during that first day. Because she didn't like seeing me all "drugged up and loopy" (as she called it) from the pain medicine I was given. There were many times when we would be having a conversation, and I would fall asleep in the middle of my sentence. It was a familiar sight to her, so she knew nothing was wrong—it was a side effect of the medicine making me zone in and out, but that horrified her to the point where she would get up and say, "OK, James, I am going to go now and let you get some rest." She made the decision to leave me there to rest, and she would come back later on that day or, if it was too late, come back in the morning when the initial shock from all the medicine had worn off. Her favorite line was, "James, you get some rest, and I will see you in the morning."

With sickle cell, our bodies are often battle tested in every way imaginable and put through so much pain, distress, and suffering and we are forced to endure it all. We have no choice if we want to survive this illness, so somehow we have to find a way to bounce back. I know the pain is never going to completely go away. It is always going to be there. But it will not be the cause of my demise, because I won't let it. I am fighter and will fight until my last breath.

But the pain is not the only thing I have to deal with. What people don't see is the mental aspect of this illness. It can be mentality and emotionally taxing because you go through so many highs and lows, and you're in and out of pain so often, that it can just wear on you. I think if you don't have the right kind of support system around you, then this illness can take ahold of you and drag you down, through the mud to the bottom of the sea.

People think by now I am used to the pain and it is OK, but that is not true at all. Given the option, I would rather not have any pain at all. True, my body has developed a higher tolerance to the pain, and through the years I have gradually grown accustomed to the pain more and more. But what people fail to realize is that each pain is different and brings on a challenging new way to fight it.

# CHAPTER 12

# <u>SHAME</u>

Throughout my life, I had always been afraid to tell anyone I had sickle cell anemia. I didn't know how people would judge me, so I always just covered it up. I remember very vividly the time when I was seventeen years old, and I was dating this girl named Jasmine. I had met Jasmine at the mall my senior year of high school. This was my first real relationship, so when we were not both in school, we would see each other quite often. One week in the summer when we were together, unfortunately, I ended up having a sickle cell crisis and had to be admitted to the hospital and stay overnight for a few days. I was admitted to St. Joseph's Hospital, where I had gone since the age of eight when Children's Hospital became too far for my mother and me to commute on the city bus. My mother worked first shift as a preschool teacher and my father worked third shift as a welder, but neither one ever owned a car while I was growing up, so I would have to take the city bus to the hospital every time I needed to go. Whenever I had a crisis, my mother would be the one to take off work to take me to the hospital.

Many times when I was younger, I would have these late night pain crises that would force me to wake up and keep me from being able to go back to sleep. When this happened, I would go straight to my mother's room to wake her up so she could give me my pain medicine; then I would go back to my room. But after the pain had taken its toll on me, and I couldn't take it anymore, I would return once again to my mother's room to tell her I was still hurting bad.

That's when she would tell me, "James, I have to take you to the hospital." She would pick up the telephone and start checking the bus schedules. If it was too late and the buses weren't running, I would crawl into her bed and wait there in pain until the morning when the buses started running again. In some instances, when I felt like I couldn't make it to the morning when the buses started up again, my mother would call one of my aunts or uncles, or a cab service to come get us. Usually, it was my Auntie Jean coming most of the time because she had reliable transportation and lived the closest to us. She drove an unforgettable little black hatchback car that my family and her family would pile up and ride around town in during the summertime. It got us around everywhere; we would take trips to the park for family barbeques and take shopping trips in it. When she came to pick us up when I was having a crisis, I just hoped to get there quick with a smooth ride. Because every little bump in the road made my body feel the pain even more. If we were taking a cab to the emergency room, sometimes the driver would let my mother sit in the front seat of the cab, and I would lie stretched out in the backseat, face down, with my head planted in my arms until we reached the front entrance of the emergency room. My mother would quickly hop out and grab me a wheelchair, and then escort me inside so I didn't have to walk.

One day, I remember Jasmine called me and asked me to come see her so we could hang out on the weekend, and I told her I couldn't. She was taken aback by my answer since we were inseparable, like conjoined twins attached at the hip whenever we were not in school or working. That compelled her to question me as to why not. Not having the slightest urge to lie about where I was, figuring that she would have to find out someday, I simply stated that I couldn't because I was in the hospital. As she heard the words hospital and me in the same sentence, it sent her straight into panic mode and had her asking me a thousand times, "Why?" and "What happened to you?"

As I listened to her over the phone, I could hear the worry in her voice; she didn't breathe or even pause to give me enough time to answer any of her questions. One after another, the questions keep swarming off the tip of her tongue like a thousand killer bees just waiting to attack and sting me one by one. I felt unsure about what to say and do, but I didn't feel comfortable enough telling anyone I had sickle cell anemia, including Jasmine, even though we were growing closer together with each day that passed. I didn't want her to judge me and I didn't want my illness to determine our relationship. Instead of breaking down and letting her in on my secret, I made up a generic excuse like I always did when my back was against the wall and I didn't want the truth about my illness to escape. I just told her I got a little heat exhaustion from the sun because I stayed out in it too long without drinking enough water and tried to leave it at that. I always made up an excuse, time after time for being sick. It never failed. But Jasmine was a very intelligent girl and I could tell that answer didn't sit well with her. I could just picture the gears in her head grinding harder and harder while she kept pressing on about the heat exhaustion thing, but I remained strong and held my stance on it.

The next day, she came to see me with her brother, Chris. Chris was a couple years younger than we were and very quiet around me when I first met him, but by this time I had gotten to know both of them very well. On the day they strolled into my room, I was in the middle of playing video games while I lay in the hospital bed, hooked up to an IV. The sixth floor was the children's floor, so there were things like movies and video games to keep kids entertained and make their stay in the hospital a little easier to cope with. Even at the age of eighteen, I was still being admitted to the sixth floor since I still had a pediatric doctor. Oftentimes, when I got bored I would ask the nurse to play the video game or watch a movie, and the nurse would wheel in this enormous steel cart with a TV mounted on it. The way it looked reminded me of the ones my teachers used in school. Everything was already connected, so all I had to do was press play. That was how I would pass the time away as the fluids, antibiotics, and medicine I needed dripped into my veins slowly from the IV.

During their visit we all just sat back and relaxed as we talked randomly about different things we wanted to do and places we wanted to go for the summer. One of my personal favorites was Six Flags Great America, near Milwaukee. Even though I was afraid of heights, I loved rollercoaster rides, and I enjoyed the thrill of the rollercoasters going up and down, with the wind hitting my face at breakneck speeds. During their stay, we also laughed a lot, and I played Chris in the video game that was sitting there. No one mentioned my stay at all. They didn't even seem to mind me being in the hospital. I guess to them it was no big deal. Still I was shy and embarrassed to let anyone I knew outside of family see me in a condition where I was sick. It made me very uncomfortable—I didn't want people to see that side of me.

The IVs did not bother me as much as when I had to wear the stupid oxygen around my face. The tube to receive oxygen would go in my nostrils and around my ears, which made it very uncomfortable. It was annoying, because the tube would get tangled everywhere. Whenever I had to get up, I would have to take it off and try to stop it from falling on the floor, getting lost between the sheets, or getting tangled up with everything else connected by some sort of cord. It was just a mess. I also thought wearing it made me look ridiculous, and I was not thrilled or amused to have it on. As a kid, it was something I always saw older people wearing to help them breathe better when they were in a poor state of health, so I didn't want their reality to become my fate. Besides, I was certain that it made me look like a circus clown, and I also thought everyone would be staring at my oxygen mask feeling sorry for me, so I just wanted to do away with it. Many times when visitors came into my room who weren't family, I would quickly snatch it off (against doctors' orders) and leave it on the bed until they left the room. I was so glad I didn't have to wear it at every hospital visit, and that was a good thing because it meant my oxygen levels were good. Although many times it was used as a precaution to keep my cells from sickling further and get my body through a crisis faster, I wanted nothing to do with it, and whenever I didn't have to wear it my spirits were high. When Jasmine came to visit, I would take it off and leave it off until she left so I wouldn't look as sick in front of her and to keep her questions about my stay down to a minimum.

The following day, she came to see me around the same time again, only this time she came by herself.

However, my reaction to her coming to see me was a hell of a lot different, because I would not grant her permission to enter my room. I was very upset that she had invited herself and that she didn't call me beforehand to let me know she was coming. That was a big deal to me. I thought, "What if I was in pain and had to take medicine in front of her? How would she act toward me if I wasn't as coherent as I was the day before?" Plus, when I was in pain I mainly just slept all day, so I didn't want to have company just watching me sleep. I wanted to be prepared for her visit as much as possible because I didn't want her to see or hear anything that could possibly reveal my condition to her. Not to mention that most of the time when I was sick, I tended to be very withdrawn and just wanted to be left alone.

The way my admission was set up, people who wanted to see me but were not on my guest list had to stop at the nurses' desk and be buzzed in to get access to my room. They would check in at the nurses' desk, and the nurse would call my room to ask me if it was OK for them to visit. If I said, "Yes," the nurse would unlock the door and buzz them in. But if I said no, she would explain to them that they were not listed as a guest, and they would be turned away. I think it was a security thing, since I was on a children's floor, but I didn't mind because I always knew who was coming to visit me.

On this particular afternoon, when Jasmine stopped by at the nurse's desk to get permission to enter my room, it was a surprise to me as I was not expecting her to be there again. The nurse called me and said, "James, you have a visitor named Jasmine here to see you. Would you like to let her in?"

My reply was a blunt, "No!" as the little voice inside my head was saying, "Why didn't she call me or let me know she was coming back? At least I could have got in the mood to have her company."

So the nurse said, "OK, I will let her know," and that was it. I didn't even see a shadow of her on that day because of my own directions.

Later, she called me, and she was irate. Her tone of voice was so loud, I held the phone off of my ear for a minute, and I could still hear her yelling as she went on complaining to me about how she could not gain access to my room. I told her I was not sure why they didn't let her in this time, and that it was probably a mistake on their part. She never knew it was me who would not grant her permission to come in to see me, as she continued to be upset and blame the hospital staff. I felt terrible about it afterward, but I did not like the fact that she had come unannounced.

In retrospect, I thought, "How could I be so self-absorbed and turn someone away that cared enough about me to come see me?" I felt a little guilty afterward when the dust had settled and I had enough time to think rationally, but at that moment I did not care because I only thought about myself and my own feelings. After all, this was the way I handled being ashamed of sickle cell. It was a perpetual state of dodging the questions about it, because I didn't want anyone to know anything about it, nor did I want anyone to find out that I had it. It left me in a constant state of running away from who I was just to be "normal" and fit in with everyone else.

When I was in the hospital, I felt like it put me in a very vulnerable state, so I wanted to keep this secret hidden. I needed to make sure the coast was clear, so nothing could be lying around with "sickle cell" on it. I didn't want to be found out yet, as I was not ready to share it with the world. In the long run, I hurt myself more than I hurt anyone else because I kept it bottled up inside me for so long with no one to turn to, and that alone made me stressed, angry, and mildly depressed. No one else had a clue what I was dealing with on the inside except for me.

I think a lot of times we forget that we are not superhuman, and that we can't take on the world by ourselves. It is impossible. We need those outside forces to help us get through tough times, and people we can talk to for support, no matter if they are going through the same thing as us or not. But I believe if we want to live a life worth living, eventually we will have to reveal ourselves and be the people we really are. I think it only takes finding that one individual we can trust and confide in. But if we choose not to be the people we wish to be, and never open up, it's only a matter of time before we will just break down and crumble like a giant cookie.

A couple days after I got released from the hospital, I went over to Jasmine's house to spend time with her like I always did. Her mother, Rhonda, was sitting on the couch with her husband, Ernest, having an intimate conversation when I walked through the door. As soon as I stepped inside the house, everything came to a screeching halt as they both acknowledged me and asked me how I was doing since being released from the hospital. I told them I was fine.

Rhonda persisted, and asked me, "What was wrong? Why were you in the hospital in the first place?"

I hated that question, no matter how it was asked. It always felt too intrusive to me because I never wanted to tell anyone I was in because of my sickle cell. I said, "I just had to be admitted because of the heat." It was the same thing I had told Jasmine days earlier when we talked on the phone before she had come to see me.

Jasmine's mother looked at me and said, "Boy, you get sick a lot. We have to figure out a way to stop that."

Ernest intervened with a comment of his own saying, "James, have you ever been tested for sickle cell?"

That could have been a chance for me to tell the truth, since it was mentioned by someone other than me. But I still chose to keep it to myself, since I was still too ashamed to admit it. I said, "No," and brushed it off.

Ernest went on to say that he had had a friend in school who had a brother with sickle cell. He said, "One week he would be feeling, fine running around playing basketball with us, and the next week he would be laid up in the house like he was dying from so much pain. He could barely move, and it was hard for me to see that."

I could tell he indeed knew about sickle cell. Then, out of concern for me, he suggested that I should get tested for sickle cell in the near future. Little did they know I was living every day with sickle cell, dealing with the exact same issues he had just described. When I had a sickle cell crisis, the pain was so unbearable and ran so deep in my flesh that it just left me paralyzed on the couch until it was all over.

That day I left their house the same way I came in, without them knowing any more about me than they already knew. Instead of taking the opportunity to open up and talk about my health, I changed the subject to something less personal and more lively until it was time for me to walk back out of the door.

That relationship lasted about five months, with me hiding my condition from Jasmine until she relocated to a different state for school. Although she never knew the reason for my stints in the hospital or why I was sick, whenever we saw each other it was never brought up, so that made things easier on me.

# CHAPTER 13

## **FINDING ACCEPTANCE**

$A$s I turned eighteen, I begin to look at having sickle cell a little differently, and I started to take it hard. It saddened me because I had friends who were preparing to go off to college, while others were leaving their parents' nest and moving out on their own, working full-time jobs and becoming more independent, while I felt like I was not. I was very happy for them, but at the same time when I looked at my own situation, I felt as if I would be left drifting along slowly, or even worse, I would be stuck in the same position because of my health. It was a bitter feeling to have. As it was, sickle cell already had a way of interrupting my daily life with all of the unpredictability that went along with having it and the disruption it caused me by having to stay in the hospital for days when I went into an uncontrollable pain crisis.

To avoid feeling any more bitterness, I just tried not to think about it. Over and over again, I told myself that I could not compare myself to anyone else. But at that age it was hard for me not to, especially since everyone around me wanted to compare me to my peers. I let the doubts I had seep into my brain, and I began to look at my future with a lot of uncertainty. It was like I was staring through the fog down into a dark tunnel. As human beings, it's a natural thing for us to compare ourselves to others, to make ourselves feel better or to see how we are doing as we go through different stages in our life. But when others are constantly comparing you to someone else to see where you fit in in this world, that gets under my skin, and I hate it the most because we are all different.

During my senior year of high school I said, "Fuck it!" and I started to rebel against my illness. I was fighting with myself on the inside, and it showed on the outside because I constantly went through different mood swings. Along with that, I wore my emotions on my sleeve more often than not, and I had a negative attitude toward having sickle cell. Many nights, I sat alone in my bedroom thinking about all of the things that I couldn't do, like try out for the high school football and basketball teams, go out of state for college, or even travel like I wanted to, and this only troubled me more. At times, it was like I lived in fear of my sickle cell because I was afraid to go anyplace new. What would I do if had a crisis and the people around me didn't know what to do or how to treat me? I could be in trouble. So I stayed away from certain places and things that would put me in that position.

As my perception of the world became more negative, and my behavior turned more erratic, so did the friends I hung around. On more than one occasion I would ride the bus to school, but when I got there, I would leave with friends so that I could go drown my sorrows with a bottle of vodka. Alcohol was the worst thing for my health, because it caused fluid loss and dehydration, and that combination was a trigger for a crisis and severe pain. But quite frankly, I started not to care anymore about what happened to me, and it was becoming more evident as the weeks passed.

Despite the disappointment in me felt by others, I wasn't taking my health seriously. I started missing my scheduled doctor's appointments. Dr. Ford, my doctor at the time, was also taking notice of my actions, and he was becoming more and more fed up over this. During one appointment, he threatened not to see me anymore as a patient if I kept up with these shenanigans. That was the one thing that I couldn't have happen, because I was going on a new medicine soon, so it was urgent that I followed up with him regularly. And I needed to have a primary physician to care for me.

I felt like with everything the doctors knew about sickle cell, there should be more done for us. I also felt like none of the doctors were doing enough for me as a sickle cell patient. I had a medicine cabinet full of prescription drugs that I took reluctantly. I questioned whether or not they would even help me. In fact, I hated taking medicine. I didn't even like to take my pain pills, because they left my stomach hurting and feeling queasy the next morning—and I didn't want to become addicted to them but in order to relieve my pain, I had to take them. In the house one time, I remember being so upset and angry about it that I shouted out things like, "I am sick of taking these stupid pills! I'm not a fucking guinea pig!" This made everyone in my family furious, because they knew the importance of my health, and they couldn't bear to watch me be so naïve and irresponsible about it. Still, at that point I couldn't have cared less. I was like a teenager rebelling against all authority when it came to my health.

As the weeks went by, I continued to cause a stir in

the home. The next thing I did was bring home a pack of cigars with the intention of smoking them until they were all gone. It was like I was trying to run my health straight into the ground. Smoking is bad for anyone, but especially someone who has sickle cell because it decreases the oxygen level in the lungs. It could cause lung infections and permanent lung damage! Even though I knew the effect it could have on me, I still decided to go to the store and pick up some cigars. When I got home, I left them on top of my dresser in plain sight for my mother to see. When she discovered them in my room, I knew it just broke her heart into pieces.

While holding back the tears in her eyes, my mother stormed out of my room and yelled to my dad, "You need to go and talk to James right now! Because I don't know what's going on with him!"

My dad came storming into my room to talk to me and try to make sense of what was going on. There was just more going on than people had enough time for, and if they sat down and talked to me, it would not have made a difference because it was something that couldn't be fixed. I was simply struggling with being an adult with sickle cell and had to come to grips with it on my own terms.

Days later, the news had spread like wildfire to my grandmother, and I received a call from her immediately. My grandmother was an easy going church woman, who always kept her bible with her and attended church service regularly throughout the week. On Sundays, she would try to encourage all of her children and grandchildren to go to church with her, and she could be seen wearing a flamboyant colored dress with a big fancy hat to match it. She was one of the first people to teach me the importance of life. She would often sit down with my family and preach to us that, "All things could be healed over time," and "No matter what you go through, you must always have faith that things will get better."

Big Momma, as we called her, was also a very funny woman. I remember riding in the backseat of her car one morning as we drove past a cemetery. She looked at me, and then pointed to the cemetery and said, "How many people do you think are dead over there?"

I took a wild guess and said, "Two hundred."

She turned back to look at me again, grinning, and said, "All of them!"

I couldn't believe it! It was so funny I was doubled over with tears from laughing so hard. I'd like to think that's where I got some of my sense of humor. Big Momma called me her "fox," and she was such a very special person to me. Anyone she came into contact with could instantly form a connection with her.

During our conversation over the telephone that evening, she told me the story of her late cousin, Julius. She said, "He didn't take his medicine or go see the doctor like he was supposed to, and one night he went to bed not feeling well and that was the last time I saw him." Tragically, Julius had passed away, and she never wanted to see me end up like that. It was enough to scare me and make me not take life for granted. She knew in her heart that I was smarter and better than how I was acting, so it saddened her to see me not caring.

My grandmother was a very loving person with a great sense of humor, and she would do anything for any one of her children or grandchildren. My favorite thing she did for us was bake us her delicious caramel cake on our birthdays and holidays. It was so mouthwatering that I devoured it within minutes. As I continued to listen to her speak, it was enough to move me, as her final comment was, "Be grateful for everything that you have." At the time, my grandmother was the only one who could reach me, and I was glad that she was there for me. We would have many conversations, but this was the first one of its kind and a very heartfelt one for me. It was a very short conversation, but that's all I needed to hear from her because anything she said to me resonated so much; I could sense the love she had for me. Her love was so unconditional. It was enough to keep me pushing forward with my head up.

When you're a kid with sickle cell, there's so much help for you and you receive so much attention when it comes to your medical condition that you always feel like you're in good hands. You never really feel like you're lost or forgotten because there are many different outlets that give you hope, inspiration, and support. But for an adult, those same support systems and that kind of medical attention are not there. I think that's the reason why it's so hard to transition from being a kid to an adult with sickle cell. It seems like when you're a kid, everyone feels sorry for you and tries their best to make you feel comfortable and fight this illness with you. But as you become an adult, everyone wants to challenge your situation and how you really feel. You have people say things to you to make you feel like you're not being tough enough about your illness. Or you're not sick; you're just looking for attention. Or you're trying to use the medicine for your personal use. It doesn't matter how strong you are—when you have to hear things like that, it can make you feel very rejected and cause you to become angry, upset, and hostile toward everyone. It was like being in two different worlds.

On the inside, my body was changing overnight. As I got older, the crises got worse and started to last longer, and the pain I was familiar with was no longer the same. I got pain in different locations all over my body that I wasn't accustomed to, and it felt ten times worse than it was before. Now that my pain was growing stronger, I needed a higher dosage of medicine to relieve it. I think as we become adults, we begin to understand that no one will be responsible for our health but us, so it's crucial that we understand our body and surround ourselves with a good support base. Because if we're not careful and we don't have a strong support group on our side, we can get lost in the shuffle and end up with poor treatment that leads to more complications and problems because of the lack of understanding and care.

# CHAPTER 14

# <u>OPENING UP</u>

**W**hen I finally summoned up the courage to speak out, the first people I told were my closest friends, Wayne and Rodney. They were brothers who lived in the same neighborhood as I did. We stayed on the north side of town next to Sherman Park, and whenever the weather was nice, we would walk up to the park to go play basketball or football. Around this time, I still had dreams of playing sports competitively so even though I couldn't play in leagues or in school, playing recreationally was one way for me to live out those dreams. Growing up, I always saw myself as being like everyone else, so I had never placed any limitations on what I could do, and it was the same with playing sports. I wanted to enjoy myself like my peers and not let my health restrict me in any way. Every time I did something, it was like I had to prove I could, and this would cause trouble for me sometimes. Because I would go so hard that I would occasionally end up pushing myself too much, to the point where I was on the verge of exhaustion. That's when I knew I would have to stop and take a break. A lot of times, when I was out playing, I wouldn't be drinking enough fluids like I was supposed to. I would be so wrapped up in what I was doing that I completely forgot about doing the necessary things like coming in the house to get a glass of water. When I was younger and gone for long periods of time, my mother would send my sister, Tanya, outside to come looking for me so that I could come in the house and get something to drink. It was her way of reminding me about my health.

When I wasn't playing sports outside with Wayne and Rodney, I spent many days over at their house hanging out and playing video games. I was over there so much, it was like I was a part of their family, and their mother treated me like her own son. Whenever we were out together, she would always tell people that I was her godson, and she invited me over for home-cooked meals on my birthday and during the holidays.

It's crazy for me to think that as much time as I spent with them all, they never once saw the sick side of me or even knew anything about what I endured as a result of sickle cell. I thought that if I told anyone I had sickle cell, they would look at me differently and treat me differently. I always wanted to be treated the same as everyone else; I didn't want people to baby me or judge me for having an illness. I feel like sometimes when you tell people you have a chronic illness, they have a tendency to treat you better in a sense or more special, and I never wanted that. So I kept it hidden and a secret between my family and me. I always looked at myself as a "normal" person rather than a person with a disability because I could do everything everyone else could do—I just had to know my limits.

One Saturday morning, I remember vividly lying in the hospital bed, talking on the telephone with my mother, contemplating whether or not I should tell my closest friends I had sickle cell. This was only a topic of discussion because I was in the hospital again, and everyone was asking about my whereabouts. Normally, I would tell my mother to tell my friends that I was at my cousin's house, and I would be home in a couple days, or I was gone, and I would call them later. But it was obvious that I couldn't keep hiding this nor did I want to anymore, so my mother didn't have to do much convincing since I knew the answer was, "Yes," they needed to know.

I knew they would be moving out of town soon, too, so this was the right time to tell them. As I lay in the hospital bed, thinking everything through, I finally came to the point where I decided to give Wayne and Rodney a call. As soon as I picked up the telephone and started dialing their number, I was hoping that they wouldn't answer so that I could prolong telling them about myself until the next time I saw them face to face. However their mother answered the telephone, so I took a breath and started off by telling her that I was in the hospital. As she listened with concern and sympathy, I reassured her that I was OK. Then I got straight to the point and told her that I had sickle cell anemia. Later on, I would speak to Wayne and Rodney to inform them also. They all said it didn't matter. They were more concerned with how I felt at the time, and said they wouldn't treat me any differently. That made me feel good, because it is hard to open up and share something personal with anyone—you never know how people will react, and you're giving them your most inner self.

Even though opening up gave me a little courage, I was not ready to go around and tell everyone else I knew. But it was a start. The moment after I broke the news over the telephone, they all were deeply concerned for me, and right away they wanted to come see me in the hospital. I declined because I was not ready to be seen, and I knew that I would be getting released soon. I was twenty-three years old when I finally told any of my closest friends I had sickle cell. I knew I would eventually tell them one day, because I could not hold this secret in any longer. It was driving me insane.

Wayne and Rodney had been there for me before in many ways, so I also felt compelled to tell them. In the end, they had suspected something might be wrong because my eyes were often jaundiced before I went on the hydroxyurea, and I would be gone for stretches of time when I was in the hospital. I decided to tell them before they moved down south to Tennessee because we had been friends for years, and it was something that I did not want to continue hiding. Ever since finding out about my sickle cell, my friends have kept my best interest in mind. Like when we have been driving for a long period of time, they will always stop at the gas station so I can pick up something to drink like water, juice, or Gatorade. If we went to the park so they could shoot baskets, they would never pressure me to play if I didn't want to. My friends have been very understanding to me, and that's very positive for me because good relationships are important to me.

Opening up also involved opening up to the women I dated. When it came to dating, I let my sickle cell interfere with my dating life like everything else. I had always had my share of girls who I dated and got along well with, but when I would have a crisis and go to the hospital, I would break all ties with them until I was feeling better. It was like I was a magician pulling off a great disappearing act right before their eyes. One minute I would be there, and the next minute—*poof*—I was gone. I was never, ever going to be in their presence while I was in my most vulnerable state, so I was never honest about my situation, and I did my best to push each one of them away. No matter how much I wanted to, I would never be around them when I was sick. I was way too uncomfortable with that because I thought that seeing me sick would make them want to abandon me like a stray cat—and abandonment was the last thing I needed in a world where I felt alone already. I only wanted the people around me who I felt secure with, and who would always be there for me. Of course, that was only my family. I wanted absolutely no contact with anyone else—not even by telephone—when I was in the hospital. But that all changed once I met Marissa.

When I met Marissa, I had already begun my hydroxyurea treatment, so my sickle cell had finally taken a back seat, and I was living my life without its painful interruptions. That made a huge difference, because I would go many months without a crisis. I was able to spend a lot of time with her and do the things I wanted to do, like taking trips out of town to different places and flying— something I had never done before.

As our relationship blossomed, and we grew closer together, I knew I wanted to open up to her and tell her I had sickle cell. Telling Marissa just felt different from telling other people. I felt compelled to speak, because I was searching for change, and right away I felt an immediate connection with Marissa, so it felt right. With her, I was definitely ready. Since my health hadn't played a part in our relationship thus far, I thought it would make it a lot easier for me to open up to her.

We had been dating for about a month when I broke my silence. Like a kid ready to finally stand up to face the schoolyard bully, I was reeling with a range of emotions. I remember sitting on the edge of my seat on the couch in the living room of my apartment as she sat next me just looking at me attentively waiting to hear what I had to say. As I begin to reveal everything about my illness, I didn't know what to expect. But her reaction to everything I had to say was a nonchalant, "OK." I didn't know how to take her response, since I was expecting more of a reaction, so I just kept talking. And everything went as smoothly as a kite sailing in the sky. She said she had heard of sickle cell, and if that was the worst thing I had to say, it was OK. From that day forward, I would continue to find different ways to tell her more information about sickle cell so she could get a better understanding of what it was and what I had to deal with.

The very first time in our relationship that I had a crisis and had to go into the hospital, Marissa was there by my side comforting me and being supportive. Because of that, my appreciation for her and her presence grew to the point where I couldn't tell her enough how it felt to have her by my side and being so understanding through it all. She was definitely a breath of fresh air, and to have her around was truly a blessing for me. As we continued dating, day by day she would slowly start to fill my mother's shoes, in a way, in terms of caring for me and my sickle cell. Every time I went to the emergency room, she stayed until the last test result came back and I was discharged by the doctor. When I had to be admitted to the hospital, she would sit with me every single day. Regardless of how she felt, she never missed a day! We ate dinner together many nights in the hospital while we watched our favorite television shows, and she would stop at stores to bring me different snacks and extra clothes from home until I was well enough to leave the hospital. I was amazed at how she juggled her schedule to fit around my care. Right after she got off of work, she would drive straight to the hospital to visit me and wouldn't rest until she got home that night. Some days I would have to tell her, "You know you can go home. I will be OK." She would still be hesitant to leave because she was so concerned. Marissa's heart was bigger than a lion's—she had the biggest heart of anyone that I had ever met.

As soon as I spoke out, a lot of things did change. I no longer felt any anger, shame, or guilt when sickle cell was mentioned. I also felt a ton of support coming from people from all over. Now when I tell people that I have sickle cell, some of the reactions I hear are, "Oh wow, I never knew you had sickle cell," or "I have a friend or a family member with sickle cell," and then they go into detail with me about some of their struggles. But the one question they all ask me is, "How does the pain feel?" That is the hardest question, because it's not easy for me to put into words to make them really understand.

People can never quite know or understand the everyday life struggles that someone goes through with sickle cell, or what it means to have sickle cell, unless they have had the misfortune of being born with it. I know everyone who knows someone with the disease just really wants to find hope or inspiration. They want to find out how to help their loved ones. I have talked for hours with complete strangers who just brought up sickle cell and wanted to know more about it. We have shared and compared stories about people they know with sickle cell so they can gain more insight from someone else who is dealing with the illness. This is good for me, because it's a chance for me to educate them on this chronic illness and answer any questions they may have.

# CHAPTER 15

# **<u>WORKING</u>**

Growing up, my father would always tell me, "James, go to school and pick up a trade so you can have a skill. That way you have more work options you can do." So after high school, that's what I decided to do. I enrolled in graphic arts at a two-year technical college in Milwaukee. I had taken a year of graphic arts in high school, but I wasn't at all psyched about it because I didn't like the whole finishing process that came with running a printing press. It was a messy process with a lot of cleaning involved, and ink would be all over me when I was finished. Also, I am a people person and found it tedious to run a noisy printing press for hours in a shop, watching it feed paper through rotating cylinders all day long. But it was the only thing that I had any knowledge and experience in, so I gave it a shot. During my first semester in school, I missed considerable time because I was also trying to work part-time to support myself, and it all took a toll on my body. I ended up having many sickle cell crises and had to be hospitalized more than once. That's when I was forced to make a decision. Either I would work now and focus on school later, or I would go to school and quit work for the time being. I chose the latter. After the first time I missed classes because of a crisis, I informed all my professors so they could be aware of what was going on with me. Afterward, my shop professor, Mr. Leonard, wanted to have a talk with me after class in private one afternoon.

Mr. Leonard was a very thin, tall man in his fifties from Chicago. He was always very animated when he spoke. As I listened to him it was like I was watching a conductor of an orchestra because his arms flailed above his head in a sweeping motion. In this meeting, he told me that he was well aware of what sickle cell was, and that graphic arts would be a hard profession for me to go into because of the hard labor and long hours. He wanted to help me to be successful in any way he could. The only catch was that I had to work hard at it and take it seriously. And that's what I did. Whenever I missed class because I was sick, he would allow me to come to his classroom and make up work. I always had the option to either come in early or stay late, whichever worked out better for me. During my lunch break, I would go up to his classroom, and he would show me how to run the printing press and finish up with any projects I needed. That helped me a lot, because I was able to manage my other classes, and his shop class was always open to me. Within two years under his tutelage, I received my certification in printing and publishing. Shortly after earning my certification, I landed my first printing job, and everything was going fine for me. But less than a month into the job, I discovered that my sickle cell was no match for the grueling physical labor. I worked twelve-hour shifts in the shop, with constant bending and lifting up loads of paper. In the end, it was just too much on my body. The overexertion kept putting me into a crisis. It was very disappointing to me because I felt like I wasted a lot of time and money on a job that I couldn't perform. I also didn't want to let Mr. Leonard down, because he got me the job. The next time I spoke to him, he told me not to worry, but added, "James, if you want to stay in this profession, you should look to work in the front office."

Once I digested Mr. Leonard's honest remarks, I knew it was the beginning of the end for me in the printing world. Twenty-four hours later, I had handed in my resignation. I was never a person who let the judgments of others discourage me from doing something, because I believed I could do anything I set my mind to. But remaining in the printing industry was a farfetched idea, and I understood that. From then on, I would change jobs frequently as I searched for a profession my body could handle and where my employers understood my situation.

Sickle cell has made my work life very challenging because I am not able to work a very physical job, and when I am having frequent crises and am in the hospital, I'm unable to work at all. When I'm off work for days, it has created conflicts between my employers and me, because they didn't understand the nature of my illness and how it affects me. It always ends up being a tug of war between me and them. During interviews, I would always tell potential employers about my illness and that it was possible I could miss work because of pain from my condition. I would still get hired, and was told in the interviews that they were OK with it. They made me feel like they understood my situation. They would even thank me for letting them know up front about my health. But when I was on the job and I had to call off of work because of a crisis, the managers would throw fits. I would call off over the phone and inform them that I couldn't make it to work, and they would try and beg me to still come in. They did not understand being sick for me meant that I could not get out of bed because of the pain, so it was not at all possible for me to work when I was home in a crisis. Pain could make me miss anywhere from a day up to a week of work, if not more. And once I got out of the hospital I couldn't go back to work immediately, because my body had to recuperate to give me the strength I needed to endure a day of work. When I would return to work I would have my doctor excuses, but the managers would still discipline me.

Maintaining a job with sickle cell can be challenging, but if you're able to find a company that understands your condition, it can be managed. Right now, I'm working because my sickle cell has been managed to the point that I'm able to work. However, I am only able to work part-time due to multiple doctors' appointments. Long hours can take a toll on me and cause me to have a pain crisis. Unfortunately some people who have chronic sickle cell are unable to work full time or even at all. That's the one thing that is frustrating for me, because I know that my health equals my wealth, so I have to keep fighting to stay healthy enough to work.

Sickle cell is something that affects us greatly in every area of our lives, but it is not impossible to have success and achieve our goals. I have met many people with sickle cell, in many different fields, who are highly successful. All in all, when it comes down to us having success while working, it just may require us to find creative ways to do things. But nothing is impossible. My mother has always told me to find a job using my hands or something more suitable for me that wouldn't put too much strain on my health, and that's exactly what I have done by writing this book. I have worked since I was fifteen years old, and I plan to stay determined and continue to strive for the best despite having sickle cell!

# CHAPTER 16

# <u>HYDROXYUREA</u>

The best times of my life have come while I have been on hydroxyurea. From the moment I started taking it at the age of twenty-six, it has been effective in cutting down the number of crises I have gotten. Now I feel like I can do just about anything and I am able to be more active in life. My energy level has also picked up tremendously.

Before I was put on the medicine, it was a constant struggle for me to maintain a good red blood cell count that would keep my body from sickling and keep me out of the hospitals every other month. When I returned to the sickle cell clinic to continue my treatment, this medicine was being used on patients with chronic cases of sickle cell. Now I was being introduced to this once-experimental drug to combat my pain crisis. During my monthly appointment at the clinic, I would tell Evelyn about my emergency room visits. She would get so frustrated with the way emergency room doctors where handling my treatment that she would yell out in disgust, "Why are they transfusing you every time?"

In an effort to eliminate the transfusions along with the recurring pain episodes, we made the decision to try hydroxyurea. I started off slowly, but once Dr. Laura and Evelyn found the right dose for me and my body adjusted to the new medication, I started having fewer sickle cell crises right off the bat.

Hydroxyurea has been known to reduce the number of pain episodes and crises that someone goes through by 50 percent. This means the number of transfusions one receives will be reduced, also. With fewer transfusions, there is less chance of getting iron overload. That's not all though. Hydroxyurea also aids in the prevention of acute chest syndrome occurring in young adults and adults.

The most noticeable change I've seen while on hydroxyurea was that the whites of my eyes appeared clearer, and I became less jaundiced while going into or coming out of a sickle cell crisis. Now I barely had any jaundice at all, and that alone made me feel good. I felt like I could handle my illness more on the inside because what bothered me most about it was almost completely gone. Having jaundice has always been a hard pill for me to swallow. Now when I look into the mirror, I no longer feel ashamed at the reflection I see staring back at me. Many times, I would looked straight into my own eyes and be ecstatic to see no yellow in them. I only saw the clearness, which is something I have always longed for. After taking this new medicine, I feel like I have been given a new lease on life with some normalcy.

The effects of hydroxyurea have also made a big difference in other aspects of my life. I have been able to work more steadily and pick up extra hours. I can earn a better income because I am having fewer pain crises. With less frequent pain episodes, my trips to the hospital and emergency room have diminished drastically. The few crises I've gotten have been treated in the emergency room and as a result, the overnight stays are very rare.

The last time I walked into the emergency room at St. Joseph's Hospital, a couple of nurses who had treated me in the past regularly were astonished to see my face. Because they had not seen me in a while, I got comments like, "Wow, where have you been? I haven't seen you in months!" and "You must have really been taking care of yourself. What have you been doing?"

When I told them that it was the hydroxyurea, they gave me a funny look, like I was speaking in a different language. Working in the emergency room, they would constantly see a flow of different sickle cell patients coming in, so they would tell me about these others patients. Some were on hydroxyurea, some not. But the ones who they knew of who were on it were still in and out of the emergency room. The only explanation I can give is that their bodies must not have taken to the medicine as well as mine, which happens in some cases. For some people it just doesn't work, and they experience the same number of crises and have to be taken off the medicine, and or they stay on it but see little difference. But for me, it just worked. My body accepted this new medicine into my system, and that was a step in the right direction toward helping me and healing me. And I feel blessed because of it.

Hydroxyurea increases the amount of fetal hemoglobin in blood cells, which interferes with the sickling process and makes red blood cells less sticky. This helps decrease the frequency and intensity of painful episodes and other complications, such as acute chest syndrome. Hydroxyurea has been proven to decrease pain and other complications in kids and adults. Some children as young as eight are being prescribed the medicine. In my case, my fetal hemoglobin increased, which showed I was making great progress and that hydroxyurea was working for me and doing its job. The presence of fetal hemoglobin in my body lowers the number of sickle cells I have, so the crisis I have is lessened. This is the reason a lot of babies do not show signs of having sickle cell until about six months of age, because their fetal hemoglobin outnumbers the sickled cells. In a way, it would be sort of like having the trait where you have a presence of sickled cells in your body, but the nonsickled cells are so high there is little to no effect.

As a result I was able to start working out regularly. But even though I was feeling good, I still had to pace myself and not overdo it. I was doing cardio at a moderate rate and some light weight lifting on my own at the local fitness center. I enjoyed working out because it helped me stay in shape and kept my blood pressure down. High blood pressure runs in my family—my grandfather had it and so did my father, so I had a greater chance of getting it, which was a concern for me. Overall, I would say, I was just happy all across the board and extremely grateful that I was seeing a vast improvement in my health and in my life.

However, even with everything I have said about hydroxyurea, it is not a miracle drug. It's not a cure and the pain will still occur. Along with that, there are some possible side effects from taking the medicine. That's why every two to three months, I go to my hematologist for a regular checkups and to have my blood drawn. He checks and monitors my red and white blood cell counts to ensure that everything is functioning the way that it should be, and no irregular changes to my blood cells are taking place that could be caused by the hydroxyurea.

Since I have started taking the hydroxyurea, I have been able to be more active in life. I personally feel like it has given me a better quality of life. Now I am able to have a more "normal life," that's less interrupted by frequent painful episodes and sickle cell crises. Hydroxyurea has made me feel like a brand new person, because it has changed the way I can live my life and the things that I can do now that I wasn't able to do before, like exercising regularly, traveling more often, and just hanging out more with friends and family. It has also been a key factor in being able to stay home for months at a time, instead of being in and out of the hospital and emergency rooms all the time. Life is good. The things I couldn't imagine doing before hydroxyurea, I can do now that my pain is under control.

I have never known what it feels like to live without sickle cell. However, it felt incredible that after just a couple of months on hydroxyurea, it took effect in my body with no symptoms or side effects. The first couple of months on this medicine gave me a glimpse into a "normal" pain-free life, and I could almost imagine what being cured of sickle cell would feel like. As I continued to take the hydroxyurea, I had no pain crises for over a year, which was even more remarkable. All the things I could only dream of before are what I am now able to do. This is what I would envision my life being like without sickle cell— being totally cured of this incurable illness. Now, after all, I had a chance to feel like a brand new person, and I was able to experience what it was like to walk in someone else's shoes for a moment. For example, I got the sense of what it was like to be my brother. I could shoot some baskets on the basketball court and not feel the aches and pains of a sickle cell crisis starting to set in my arms or knees when I was finished. If I wanted to, I could also dance for hours like my sisters and not have to take any pills days later for pain. It felt incredible, and I wished my life could be like that every single day! That is why I'm a strong advocate for a cure for sickle cell anemia, so that we can break this cycle for future generations. I want to see them live life like this: pain free without the use of medications and with no worries at all.

# CHAPTER 17

# **BLOOD TRANSFUSIONS**

One way you can help someone with sickle cell anemia is by donating blood. Since many sickle cell patients rely heavily on blood transfusions to treat and prevent complications of sickle cell such as stroke, acute chest syndrome, priapism, and low blood count, donating blood helps us all out tremendously. Blood transfusions help boost our red blood cell count and eliminate sickled blood cells. People who have had sickling in the lungs or a stroke may require blood transfusions about once a month for the rest of their lives, so your contribution can be vital to maintaining their health and quality of life.

By the time I was eighteen, I had already had an inconceivable amount of blood transfusions. If you asked me to count the number of transfusions I had and give you a number, I couldn't do it. Every time my red blood cell counts got low, there was a chance that I would need one. To keep from having to be admitted to the hospital, I would go to the outpatient clinic with my mother and get a transfusion. A low red blood cell count would cause a pain episode to begin, sending me into a sickle cell crisis. Then I would have to go to the hospital and be treated.

Blood transfusions helped me because they were giving my body new red blood cells to prevent any other complications caused by anemia. Since sickle cells only last ten to twenty days compared to normal red blood cells, which circulate in the body for about 120 days, it was normal for me to have a lower red blood cell count. Because of this rapid destruction of red blood cells, my body can't make new ones fast enough, bringing on severe pain and anemia. The pain is just one symptom of sickle cell anemia.

Whenever I received a blood transfusion, I would get one or two units of blood at a time. It just depended on what the doctor felt was sufficient to raise my blood count on that particular day.

First, I would have my blood drawn by a lab tech. Next, they would match my blood with the right blood donor. Then the blood would be run through an IV into a vein in my arm. Except that it's blood instead of fluids, the transfusion doesn't feel any different from any other IV. Once the process has begun, a nurse will come into my room and check my vital signs for the first fifteen minutes of the transfusion. He or she is checking for anything unusual that could be caused by receiving this new blood, like a change in blood pressure, pulse, temperature, swelling, rashes, or anything else that could be a sign of a reaction. If everything is fine, after the first hour has passed, I can kick back and relax while the blood in the hanging bag empties out into my vein. I have been getting blood transfusions since I was about six years old, and I still have to receive them when my numbers get low enough, so people donating blood is a big deal to me because it is a key component in treating my sickle cell.

The most blood I have received in one transfusion is two units (one unit equals one bag of blood). I have only had one allergic reaction to the blood; I got a rash on my chest after receiving the blood, but it wasn't anything serious and went away shortly after. Usually a bag of blood takes about two hours to run through the IV. Having an IV in your arm can be a hindrance, depending on the location. If the IV needle is placed in my arm where the elbow bends, I can't move my arm freely, and I'm just sitting there waiting for it to be over. But all in all, it is not too unpleasant for me to deal with.

There have been a couple of times when I have had an IV in each arm at the same time: one for the transfusion and the other one for the pain medicine. When you're receiving blood, you can't have anything else going through the IV. As you can imagine, having an IV in both arms made it very difficult for me when I needed to get up out of bed and move around. If I wanted to get up and go to the bathroom, I would have to haul around both IV poles while I tried to keep my balance and not trip over my own feet and the poles. The main thing on my mind was not to accidently rip out the IV lines. It was like I was doing a balancing act with both my arms trying not to knock the two poles into each other while I maneuvered around my room. If there was ever a time when I needed an extra arm or hand this was it. However I was never shy about asking the nurse for help, especially when I was in a lot of pain. I would just push the call light connected to my bed to call the nurse for assistance.

After receiving the new blood, I notice a big difference right away; I started to feel better almost immediately. It would only take my body a day or two to feel reenergized and back to my normal self. Then the pain was gone and so was the fatigue.

Even though getting blood transfusions helps me recover and feel better faster, it is not always the answer to treating me, because getting too much blood can cause harm to your body over time. This is why many doctors monitor the number of blood transfusions you are receiving. Most doctors prefer not to continually give you blood transfusions because of the many complications that can come along with receiving too much blood.

The first complication is iron overload; the more transfusions you receive the more your body will start to build up iron from all the blood and store it inside the body. Having too much iron in your body can be toxic because there is no way to get rid of the iron. Over time, it spreads to your organs and can be fatal. The only way to remove this excess iron is by taking a pill called xjade or through a process called chelation. Excess iron can be fatal, causing heart problems, or diabetes, or liver disease. Therefore, it's crucial for people with sickle cell to know about iron overload because it's a very dangerous condition. In the past, I have had doctors avoid giving me transfusions because of concerns about iron overload. Their hope was that with the IV fluids, antibiotics, and pain medication, my body would recoup on its own, and there would be no need for me to be transfused.

Another complication from being transfused multiple times is that your body starts to develop antibodies. Each time you go for a transfusion, it makes it harder for the nurse to find a blood donor match. Once your body recognizes blood is coming from a different ethnic group, you will develop antibodies to it and will not be able to tolerate the transfusions.

It is wise for people with sickle cell to be keenly

aware of the effects of getting blood transfusions. There are doctors who do not fully understand the condition and when they see a lower red blood count, they may have the tendency to over transfuse, which could be dangerous to you. In the past I have seen many doctors in the emergency room who were inexperienced in dealing with sickle cell patients; many told me flat out that I was their first sickle cell patient or that they didn't know much about the disease.

I remember the first time I took Marissa to witness me getting a blood transfusion at the outpatient clinic. My red blood count was low, and my hematologist ordered me to have one, since I had been experiencing pain crises with low red blood counts for a while. The minute I told Marissa that I had to have this done, she started to freak out and get very worried. Her cheeks started to flush red and she asked me a bunch of questions.

She said, "A transfusion? What, why? Are you going to be OK? Do you have to stay in the hospital?" She thought it was going to be a long procedure like a surgery or something worse. I calmed her down by sitting her on the couch and letting her know that everything was going to be fine, while trying to hold in my laughter. I had been transfused many times, and I knew it was not this big ordeal that she was picturing. But it was the first time I had had to go through this since we were together. On the day of my transfusion, Marissa was quiet as we drove to the hospital. I could tell she was still a little nervous as I watched her from the passenger seat, bobbing and weaving through traffic like an ambulance until we reached the front entrance of the hospital. Once I got checked in, and she saw that it was like getting an IV for me and everything would be fine, she was finally relieved. It took a couple of hours for me to get transfused, so as a way of thanking her for being my guest, I let her be in charge of the TV. Big mistake on my part! The whole time we were there, we watched soap operas, until the last drop of blood from the bag had dripped into my vein, and I was all finished.

Because there is a high need for blood donors, and more and more restrictions to the blood supply, there is always a shortage of blood. With fewer people eligible to donate blood, those who are in need the most are greatly affected by this. Donating blood can solve some of these problems, but it has to be a collective effort.

There need to be more African American blood donors because receiving blood from another ethic group can cause a sickle cell patient to develop antibodies, making it harder to get transfused when you need it.

I think the reason there are currently not enough blood donors is because people simply are not aware of what's going on and the need for blood. Giving blood is fairly quick and easy, and it doesn't hurt at all. If you want to help, and you're not sure how to start or where to go, go to a website like www.redcross.org/blood to find a blood drive near you, or ask at a local hospital to find out where you can donate blood.

I have encouraged my family to donate blood, and they have all stepped up to the plate to donate numerous times. I am very appreciative of that. Because donating blood does not have to be a one-time thing. You can donate as often as you like as long as you're healthy enough. Since African Americans are the most afflicted by sickle cell, I would love to see more African Americans lend their support to the sickle cell community and donate. September is Sickle Cell Awareness Month and June 19 is world Sickle Cell Awareness Day, so take the time out to help someone with sickle cell. You can start by donating blood or helping with fund raising to raise money for your local organizations. You can also show your support by spreading the word and raising awareness in your community, since sickle cell primarily affects the African American community.

The key to managing this condition is getting educated about what to do if you have sickle cell anemia, and what to do to help if you don't.

# CHAPTER 18

# <u>CURES</u>

**B**one **Marrow Transplant:** Right now, the only known cure for sickle cell is a bone marrow transplant. Bone marrow is a factory for red blood cells and contains blood-producing stem cells. The procedure can only be performed if the patient finds a donor who is a perfect match, usually a sibling. If a match cannot be found within the family, they now have the option to find a donor outside of the family. Today anyone registered on the list to be a bone marrow donor can be considered as long as they are a perfect match for the patient. That could have been a real possibility for me when I was younger, because I do have a brother and two sisters, but they were never tested to see if they were compatible. I believe when my mother and father first heard about it, the procedure was still in the early stages, so they had a lot of doubts. Evelyn was the first person who ever mentioned anything to my mother or me about this bone marrow procedure. My mother and I were at a function for sickle cell when it was initially brought to our attention as a cure for my sickle cell. I was about ten years old when I heard this news, but I understood the significance of it and what it would mean for me. As you could imagine I was definitely curious about this procedure, but only minimal information was given to us. If we wanted to know more, we would have to come into the sickle cell clinic to find out more about the procedure.

The way a bone marrow transplant works is by carefully injecting the donor's bone marrow into the recipient's veins. After the bone marrow has been injected, over time it replaces the recipient's old bone marrow and starts making red blood cells. These will be nonsickled red blood cells. This procedure takes several months and can be very expensive.

Not all procedures are successful. Sometimes bone marrow transplantation does not work, and the new bone marrow is rejected in a form of immune response called graft-versus-host disease. There is a "5 to 10 percent risk of death respectively of those who go through it" according to the book *Hope and Destiny: The Patient and Parent's Guide to Sickle Cell Disease and Sickle Cell Trait* by Alan Platt. There have also been cases where people have received a transplant that did not work, and they ended up having sickle cell again. For my mother and father this definitely was out of the question. The risks outweighed the possibility of me being cured, and there would be no second-guessing their decision at all. They both wanted me to be pain free, but as they learned more about it, they felt that this was not the right procedure for me. Once the decision was made, it was never brought up again. Neither of my parents thought that they should be putting me and my siblings through this procedure. For them, the uncertainty overshadowed any possibility of this working and me being cured and having a "normal" sickle cell-free life.

With any transplant, there's a lot to think about. You have to acknowledge the very real possibility of losing a child or a loved one if the new bone marrow is rejected, so it's a very scary situation. I think the consequences of something going wrong would be too devastating and would have haunted my parents for the rest of their lives. They knew from the start that this was not a decision that was up to them to make. Instead, in these types of situations, they always said, "The best thing to do was let go, and put it in God's hands."

Generally, a bone marrow transplant is considered only for sickle cell patients with extremely severe cases. For instance, this would be recommended if the child had a stroke or lung damage caused by acute chest syndrome or very frequent severe pain crises, which required them to have monthly transfusions. Even though my sickle cell was not severe enough to require a transplant back then, I think if I knew the procedure could be performed safely, and I had the option to speak for myself, I would have jumped on that opportunity and been on the operating table before you could blink twice. Because no one in their right mind should have to go through the daily struggle and pain we face in our lives.

**Gene Therapy:** Gene therapy is on the horizon and could be the best option to cure sickle cell in the future. Scientists are working right now on a gene therapy study that would essentially correct the sickle cell hemoglobin defect in human blood cells. Unlike a bone marrow transplant, where doctors use bone marrow stem cells from a well-matched donor, gene therapy would use stem cells from the person affected with sickle cell. Scientists are trying to find a way to place a normal gene inside the body of the patient that will "auto correct" the sickle cell gene and turn it into a normal gene.

This procedure is still in the testing stages, so there is little information about the process or how this procedure could happen. For now, there are few options for those of us who live each and every day with the chronic illness. Our only hope for a cure is a bone marrow transplant. Unfortunately for children with sickle cell, the percentages are low because they have to have a brother or sister who doesn't have sickle cell and is also a compatible match. According to *Hope and Destiny*, "In general any two siblings have about a one in four chance of sharing the same HLA type." HLA stands for human leukocyte antigen, which is on bone marrow cells and is an essential element for all immune functions. It is important that this match, or there can be extreme complications or even death, because your cells will not recognize your organs and began to attack them.

With the new technology we have today and the advancements in science and medicine, I am very optimistic there will be success in finding a cure. The only question is, how long will it take?

**Awareness:** Awareness is the best cure! Right now the most effective way to stop the spread of sickle cell today is by being tested and finding out if you are a carrier of the sickle cell trait. This can be done by your health care provider with a simple blood test called hemoglobin electrophoresis.

According to *Blood and Circulatory Disorder Sourcebook,* second edition, "About 2 million Americans carry the sickle cell trait. About 1 in every 12 African Americans has the sickle cell trait." Generally people with the trait live normal healthy lives and show no signs of any symptoms. However, they may experience some of the same symptoms as a person who has sickle cell when exposed to low oxygen pressures, extreme physical activities, and dehydration since 50 percent of their hemoglobin is made up of the sickle cell gene.

If you are not aware that you have sickle cell trait, the result of overexertion can be fatal. That's why college athletes are now tested to see if they are carriers of the sickle cell trait and, if so, many are encouraged to sit out and not play. There have been a few instances where college athletes with sickle cell trait collapsed and died from overexertion.

You can also pass on the sickle cell gene if you ever decide to have children. That's why if you are serious about having children, both you and your spouse or significant other should get tested so you know what's at stake if you both carry the gene for sickle cell. Because the risks are always high to have a child with sickle cell, and the odds are always the same, a 25 percent chance for each and every birth, if both parents are carriers. In any case, it is always a good thing to know whether or not you have the sickle cell trait.

Since I have sickle cell, I know I will pass on the sickle gene if I have a child. I know I could not have children if I knew that they might be born with sickle cell. I would not want to see my children go through the same struggles and pain in life that I have. Just to look at myself in the mirror, knowing that I passed on sickle cell to my child after all that I knew about the illness, would be very hard. I think it would be downright selfish.

Having sickle cell is not an impossible thing to live with. You can still have a good vibrant life, a good future, and be active, but if you have the option to prevent it, I think you should take every measure to do so. We need your help to make sickle cell less of an issue and stop the number of babies being born with this terrible chronic illness. So let's join hands in the fight against sickle cell because with awareness and your cooperation we can all help to break the sickle cell cycle.

# CHAPTER 19

# **CONCLUSION**

Life has been a different journey for me because I have had to endure a lot of pain and suffering to get to where I am today. But because of what I went through, I'm a much stronger person. Now that I'm thirty-three years old and have lived my whole life with sickle cell, I can't imagine my life without it. It has made me become the person I am today. If I hadn't been born with it, I can't imagine who or where I would be. Like a rollercoaster, my life has been filled with many ups and downs and unexpected twist and turns, but in the end I found the strength and patience to overcome it all, to remain here, still standing.

Having sickle cell is not a death sentence; you can manage it and learn to live a happy productive life with it, as long as you choose not to let it define you. Now that I'm able to open up and talk about my illness, I feel like a heavy weight has been lifted off my shoulders. I no longer carry the burden of having sickle cell anymore, because I have accepted the things that I cannot change. The hard feelings that I once got from having sickle cell, about what others thought of me because of it, are completely gone; those people's thoughts no longer exist in my mind. Now I have taken charge of my life, and I refuse to let anyone or anything hold me back from living my life to the fullest.

The moment that I spoke out about my illness for the first time, I released so much tension that I was shaken with a jolt of energy, and I felt so liberated. Like a dove being released from a steel cage, I was finally free! I was free from myself. I was free from everything that I had kept caged and hidden deep inside of me behind these indestructible walls of my chest, and now I could just be myself. There was no more hiding or covering up that big ugly monster that resided deep in my blood and was known to me as sickle cell anemia. I now had the strength and courage to stand up and face that demon, and talk about it without feeling there would be any repercussions. Since my birth, it has lain deep within my flesh and bones, causing me nothing but pain and heartache. By rearing its ugly head and emerging time after time in the form of a sickle cell crisis, it was something I could not silence. But I would not be defeated by it. It was only a matter of time before I would eventually get this off of my chest, and overcome this.

In the end, I knew I could no longer be silent about the thing I cared about the most: helping others like myself who felt alone as they suffered in silence, praying for change. I knew if I ever wanted to see a change in the world, first I had to change and open up. One day, it finally dawned on me, because I knew the impact of me speaking out about sickle cell was far more beneficial than me choosing to remain silent. I had been in the dark for too long about my illness. Deep down, I knew if I spoke out about it, I would finally see that there was a light at the end of the tunnel for me.

I hope by sharing my story with you, I have opened up your eyes to see the seriousness of this chronic illness. My intention is not to have you feel sorry for me, but rather to inform and educate you about the significance of sickle cell. By giving you a glimpse into my life, you can see what it is like for people to live with this debilitating illness and the challenges we face each day.

Throughout this journey, I have learned a lot about myself, including that I can no longer be silent about the things that matter most to me, especially if I want to change the way other people view sickle cell. While there may still be some people who will continue to ignore this chronic illness, I truly believe that one day we will reach everyone who matters the most. With the grace of God and advanced medicine, we will have a cure for sickle cell.

Until then, I will continue to smile, fight, and live my life to the fullest each day. Because I know that even behind the darkest clouds the sun is still shining bright as ever!

# <u>REFERENCES</u>

Garrison, Cheryl D., and Charles M. Peterson, *The Iron Disorders Institute Guide to Anemia*. (Nashville: Cumberland House, 2003), 249–261.

Gibbons, Gary H., "Who Is at Risk for Sickle Cell Anemia?" National Institutes of Health. Department of Health and Human Services, accessed September 8, 2014, http://www.nhlbi.nih.gov/health/health-topics/topics/sca/atrisk.html.

Platt Jr., Allan F., and Alan Sacerdote. *Hope and Destiny: A Patient's and Parent's Guide to Sickle Cell Disease and Sickle Cell Trait*. Roscoe, IL: Hilton, 2002. 177-194.

Shannon, Joyce Brennfleck, ed. *Pain Sourcebook*. 3rd ed. Detroit: Omnigraphics, 2008. 301–309.

Sutton, Amy L., ed. *Blood and Circulatory Disorders Sourcebook*. 2nd ed. Detroit: Omnigraphics, 2005. Section 10.1–10.2.

# ABOUT THE AUTHOR

James Griffin III lives in Phoenix, Arizona, with his wife, Marissa, and their Boston Terrier, Destiney. He is involved with numerous sickle cell organizations and support groups; in 2011, he had the chance to participate in his first Walk for Sickle Cell to help raise money and awareness for the cause. To stay on top of his health, he exercises daily, maintains a healthy diet, and goes to a sickle cell outpatient clinic a couple of times a month. In his leisure time, he loves listening to music, watching football, and spending time with his wife and dog. His mission in life is to continue spreading sickle cell awareness through his writing, sickle cell organizations, and other outlets.

James Griffin III can be contacted at:
Email: jamesgriff3@yahoo.com
Facebook: https://www.facebook.com/james.ace.21
Twitter: @jamesace21

Made in the USA
Monee, IL
02 June 2023

34758557R00085